'What Were You Arguing About Along the Way?'

Gospel Reflections for Advent, Christmas, Lent, Holy Week and Easter

From the Spirituality of Conflict Project

'What Were You Arguing About Along the Way?'

*Gospel Reflections for Advent,
Christmas, Lent, Holy Week and Easter*

From the Spirituality of Conflict Project

Edited by Pat Bennett

Introduction by Pádraig Ó Tuama

CANTERBURY
PRESS
Norwich

© Contributors 2021

Published in 2021 by Canterbury Press
Editorial office
3rd Floor, Invicta House,
108–114 Golden Lane,
London EC1Y OTG, UK
www.canterburypress.co.uk

Canterbury Press is an imprint of Hymns Ancient & Modern Ltd
(a registered charity)

Hymns Ancient & Modern® is a registered trademark of
Hymns Ancient & Modern Ltd
13A Hellesdon Park Road, Norwich,
Norfolk NR6 5DR, UK

Scripture quotations, unless otherwise indicated, are from the New Revised
Standard Version of the Bible, copyright 1989 by the Division of Christian
Education of the National Council of the Churches of Christ in the USA.
Used by permission. All rights reserved.
Scripture quotations marked (CEV) are from the Contemporary English
Version Copyright © 1991, 1992, 1995 by American Bible Society.
Used by Permission.
Scripture quotations marked (ESV) are from The ESV® Bible (The Holy Bible,
English Standard Version®), copyright © 2001 by Crossway, a publishing
ministry of Good News Publishers. Used by permission. All rights reserved.

British Library Cataloguing in Publication data

A catalogue record for this book is available
from the British Library

978-1-78622-399-9

Typeset by Regent Typesetting
Printed and bound by
CPI Group (UK) Ltd

Contents

Advent Year C

The Nativity of the Lord – Years A, B and C

Reflections for Ash Wednesday and the Season of Lent

Lent Year A

Lent Year B: 'Private and Public' – Lent-themed Series

Reflections for Holy Week and Easter

Liturgy of the Passion

Holy Week

'The Spaces We Inhabit' – Holy Week-themed Series

The Resurrection of the Lord

Easter Evening

Easter 2

Acknowledgements

We wish to extend our heartfelt gratitude to the following for their generosity and support of the Spirituality of Conflict project. Some of these organizations gave financially to our writing retreats, others gave staff time, all gave support, insight and wisdom.

The Trench Trust, whose imagination and generosity started this project off
The Corrymeela Community
The Iona Community
Place for Hope
Coventry Cathedral
The Irish School of Ecumenics
The Mission and Discipleship Council of the Church of Scotland
The Parish of Holy Island, Northumberland
The Church of Scotland
The thousand weekly readers of the emails – your feedback and kindness has helped shape this project

Our project has always been built around writers from across Britain and Ireland coming together to share and learn from each other, to be with each other in conflict and community, to write from an experience of friendship and tension, and to bring the gospel texts into conversation with what we know of working for peace through the conflicts of our world. As such, this has always felt more than a writing group. There have been some people who've been part of the group for six months, others for a year, others since it started, others more recently. Everyone has contributed so much to this, and we are grateful for their work, especially Jude Thompson and

Graham Fender-Allison who formed such a vital part of the group in the early years of the project.

Our dear and beloved friend Glenn Jordan joined the group a few years into it, and within an hour everyone felt as if they'd been known by him for years. He was a repository of insight and delight, wisdom and warmth. He died unexpectedly in June 2020. We loved Glenn, and were loved by him. His name is a blessing.

Introduction

Pádraig Ó Tuama

Years ago, I was at a conference where people argued about language. It wasn't a conference for poets, editors or linguists – although many people there wrote poetry, edited texts and thought about language – it was a conference about conflict. Or, perhaps it's more accurate to say it was a conference about peace. Or, again, perhaps it's accurate to say that it was a conference about conflict and peace, because each relates to the other. Whatever the conference was about, there was an argument about language. Someone had given a talk about Peacebuilding. And someone replied they didn't like the term *building* at the end of Peace*building*. Thereupon a long conversation ensued. And it wasn't a silly one, it was a serious one. So when someone said they didn't like the idea of Peace being *built* they were making an important point. They said that if you think Peace is built, then you need to have a conversation with an engineer, or designer, or architect, you need to think about the cement, the foundations, and you need to think about the fact that buildings don't build themselves.

Peace, someone at the conference said, is less like a building, and more like something that grows. Sure, it can be supported in its growth, but *we*, the person said, are not the ones who designed it, merely the ones who hopefully help it – or, at least don't impede it – and who, moreover, benefit from it.

Peacecultivation, someone suggested. Peaceseeding, someone else said. Peacenurturing someone said. I liked all the ideas, especially the agricultural ones.

All this can seem like an echo of a crowd of entitled people arguing semantics while wars rage. But they weren't. Plenty of the people expressing opinions had lived through atrocious threat, bereavement, loss, terror, marginalization and exploitation. People in that room had been shot at, recruited into organizations that required them to kill, were injured, imprisoned; people in the room had fought for peace (oh, yes, the irony), had lost friends because of their engagement with reconciliation, and had wondered how this fragile hope they had could ever take root.

And we're back in the earth again. Take root. Grow. Cultivate.

All of this goes to say that peace is only abstract for people for whom it's abstract. Peace, when you're trying to find it (build it, grow it, make it, keep it) requires a lot. And, to visit the land of irony again, peace requires a lot of conflict. Not just as the initial chaos that is being addressed but also along the way. Groups that work collaboratively for peace are usually in conflict, sometimes explicitly, often implicitly. This isn't a mark of irony, it's a mark of the good work. To seek peace – now we're on a map – we must be willing to face the thing that is causing the need for peace-seeking: conflict.

I've often quoted Claire Mitchell's brilliant phrase about the British–Irish conflict being a *meta*conflict, because there's 'conflict about what the conflict's about'. That's true, no less so since Brexit, but there's more too. There's conflict about what peace looks like, and not just here, everywhere. Take a group of people who are having an argument and ask them what a good resolution will look like: one will say that things will go back to what they were before; someone else will say that no, the way things were before was like pre-conflict, with all the settings for what became inevitable; someone else will say that they just want to win; someone else will say that they wish their enemies to be destroyed; someone else will say they're willing to accept compromise; and someone else will be worried about something else entirely.

Again – I know I'm repeating myself, I'm sorry, I hope it's not causing you upset – peace is full of conflict.

'What were you arguing about along the way?' Jesus of Nazareth asked his followers. They'd been arguing but were now silenced, because the question asked plunged them into even more conflict. Their conflict was one that was worthy of more than silence, though; their conflict was the serious stuff of living: who are we? What are we doing following this man? What matters? What do I do with my ambition? What does he think is of value? What do I think is of value in what he thinks is of value? And anyway, who's he when he's at home? Without that conflict we would not have the image of Jesus taking a child – whose child? his own, I like to think – embracing it and speaking powerfully about hospitality in response to his followers' hostility. These followers were not following. They're not pantomime fools either, they are all of us. It is hard to know what to see when seeing is hard to do. *Kyrie eleison.*

Most groups manifest the opposite of the thing they say they're for. It's a horrible truth, but it's often true. So, a communications company will, for instance, often fail at internal communications. A harmony group might be discordant. Prayer groups can have whatever the opposite of prayer is happening among them. And peace groups are filled with conflict. The trick is not to see this through only one lens. It's easy to think that a conflict-ridden peace group is manifesting either ineptitude or duplicity. But I don't think that's a good enough analysis. In fact, after years working in conflict, if I meet a peace group who have no conflict among them, I begin to wonder what the element of quiet threat or control is that's operating among them. I want to see groups in conflict, because if anything is worth conflict, peace is. And peace groups that can face their own conflicts are groups that might have something to say. However, what often happens is that peace groups experience conflict, they see their conflict as a demonstration of hypocrisy, they splinter, and the members go elsewhere. And then those who remain have a story to tell about how they're a better peace group now that the others are gone. And that starts a new story. And new people who join hear about the people who left. And the story continues.

Somehow, though I do not know you, I know you have experienced this. Me too. Sometimes I've been the one who has left. Sometimes I've been the one who has stayed. Often,

I've been the one who has joined a little late, so I hear stories about those ~~bastards~~ people who left.

Oh, the things unsaid.

The Spirituality of Conflict project started because of a conflict. Someone wrote to me saying that all my peace and reconciliation talk – I was leading Corrymeela at the time – was missing the point. For them, the reconciliation we needed was with God, not each other. If we sort out the God stuff, then that's the main priority sorted, they said. This isn't a caricature. They wrote it. I thought about this a lot, actually. I wondered who the person was – they wrote an anonymous tweet that's long since been deleted. I wondered what it was about their faith that was so important for them to speak. I wondered about how they'd tell their story of anonymity. And I wondered what conflicts they were in – with friends, or family, or neighbours or fellow congregants. I'd been thinking for a while that I'd like to work with a group of people on a project that explored conflict through the lens of the gospel texts and this seemed like a fine reason to start.

The centuries of British–Irish conflict are too long to go into here. But I knew that I wanted this project to have membership from groups across Ireland and Britain. So, I went about writing to groups – Iona, Place for Hope, Coventry, the Church of England, the Church of Scotland, Irish Catholics and Protestants, ordained people, lay people – asking who had interest and time in being part of a writing group who would write reflections on the Sunday gospel readings, reflections that would engage with the experience and reality of conflict in our lives. Fast forward lots of emails, memoranda of understanding, discussions as to whether the term *partnership* was usable because the lawyers from some groups disliked the term organizational *partnership*, and there were seven of us in a room at Corrymeela, talking about this idea.

Of all the ideas we had, only a few remain: we are a group of people from across Britain and Ireland who write about conflict and the gospels. We do so in a spirit of friendship and connection. Our retreats – when we can afford them – are filled with laughter, discussion, disagreement, long long meals, fireplaces, walks, prayer, reflection and sea-swimming. Some people have been in the group since the beginning. Others have left. Others have changed jobs but stayed in the writing group. New people have arrived. One – Glenn Jordan – has died (we carry him in our hearts; we carry his heart in our hearts).

We are in our fifth year of writing at this stage, with about 1,500 people receiving weekly emails exploring how spirituality and conflict can be part of something creative in the human endeavour. We do not always agree with each other as a group, and this has been a great joy, even if it means some of our meetings need to be long. In any gathering of people there will be tensions, conflicts, ways that old shadows cast new shadows. We, like any group who experience the some-times-surprise of tension, start with bewilderment in these moments. But as the years have gone on, I've noticed, too, the ways an intelligence of conflict is practised in the group. Some people clearly choose what it is that's worth arguing about. And that's a wisdom. Others have found private moments for discussion and deepening of relationships. And that's a wisdom too. Some of our arguments remain as creative tensions. And that's wisdom as well. And some arguments reflect something bigger than we have the words for: foundational plates that move and cause creaks on the surface. There, we fill our plates with food and conversation. Whatever conflict is, hospitality is always a wise response.

Did I say wise? I think I meant spirit, by which I mean breath, by which I mean survive. By which I mean, yes.

Conflict is bewildering; whether it happens in a family, a congregation, an organization, a country. It's like being dropped in a location for which you have no map and where the landscape is changing all the time anyway. Ten things are happening at once and each of those ten things has a different piece of insight: stay, go, stop, return, plough on, dig deep, reflect, act. Then there's conflict about how to get out of conflict – thank you, Claire Mitchell – and some people are focusing on solutions while others are grieving, others are traumatized and others don't think they're lost at all. Alliances form and break. Enmities cement and crumble. The first day.

In all of this, what we propose is simple: a spirituality, a breathing capacity for those moments. We do not propose solutions – peace and conflict are not easy and take love, time, risk and skill – but we do believe that the gospel texts have some wisdoms to share. And we also believe that our lives, friends from across Ireland and Britain, have something to share, even if only in stories of how we've tried to find a map, how we've tried to learn from the things we argue about along the way, how we prayed we could find a good solution and make that solution last, how we practised. These offerings come from the place of brokenness that conflict can sometimes open up in us: brokenness from our own lives, brokenness from grief, brokenness, too, from the larger historical and political factors that rage all round us. Given these brokennesses, we do what we know to be good: we talk, we try, we disagree and argue, we pray, we learn, we collaborate, we practise hospitality, we take walks, we grow in love and we practise the thing we hope will sustain us: breathing.

Exploring the Space Between
Introducing a Spirituality of Conflict
Pat Bennett

Where there is separation
there is pain.
And where there is pain
there is story.
And where there is story
there is understanding
and misunderstanding
listening
and not listening.
May we turn toward each other,
and turn toward our stories,
with understanding
and listening,
with argument and acceptance,
with challenge, change
and consolation.
Because if God is to be found,
God will be found
in the space
between.
Amen.[1]

When the search is centred on a definite object, as in prospecting, everything that is not this object is dismissed as irrelevant. For the explorer, on the other hand, everything that comes into view is in some way welcome and appears as a sort of gratuitous gift which is like an enrichment for him [*sic*] who finds it and receives it.[2]

The idea that there could, or indeed *should*, be a connection between spirituality and conflict is not necessarily one that sits easily at first. Indeed, the very concept of a 'spirituality of conflict' might at best feel slightly jarring, at worst offensively oxymoronic: why not a spirituality of peace or a spirituality of reconciliation – surely these would be more in keeping with what we take to be the message of the gospel? However, when we consider that conflict is a ubiquitous feature of human life and that spirituality, in its many different conceptions, is essentially an important map by which people explore, order and give meaning to their life-world, the coupling suddenly seems not just less contentious but in fact one that is vitally important. Moreover, while reconciliation and peace are the goals for which we strive, that journey is rarely an abstract philosophical one – it arises out of the lived reality of our own experiences of conflict.

Such experiences, if we are able to step back and examine them, can reveal much that is at the heart of our own personal understandings: the maps by which we navigate the world and negotiate our relationships; the way we fashion our identities and frame our stories; the desires that define our choices and drive our actions; the spaces within which we habitually operate and the extent to which these constrain or expand the possibilities for dialogue and action. The more we are able to see and understand these contours and dynamics, the more we will be able to engage with the conflicts we inhabit and encounter in constructive ways – ways that add depth and nuance to our understandings and enlarge our vocabularies and grammars of speech and action, thereby increasing the potential for new possibilities of peace and flourishing. At the heart of the Spirituality of Conflict project is the conviction that the gospel texts have a wealth of deep wisdom to offer us in this quest, and not just in those places where the texts directly address conflict themselves: there are insights to be found across the whole richly textured panoply of the gospels as they address key questions about what it is to be human, to be in relationship, to love and serve God, to resist injustice and to live the full, generous and hospitable life which Jesus comes to announce and embody.

We have a tendency to assume that the experience of conflict is synonymous with damage and destruction and thus something to be avoided or minimized at any price. This, though, is to miss the vital point that conflict can also have important creative potential. Just as short-term stressors play an important role in adaptive up-regulation of various body systems, so too conflict, in calling us to reassess how we engage and interact with both individuals and systems, can be an important factor in the development of new understandings and patterns of thought and behaviour. However, this positive potential should never lead us to lose sight of the destructive aspects of conflict and its propensity to cause pain and disruption at personal, community and systemic levels: human lives bear the cost of conflict; moreover, such costs are often very disproportionately distributed. Any spirituality of conflict faithful to the Gospel must necessarily be one which shines a light on the structural and systemic narratives of power and violence that suppress and demean people, on the possibility and extent of our own complicity in these, and on where there is need for resistance and change.

But while it is important to recognize that conflict has both positive and negative aspects, we also need to move beyond this simple binary. Conflict is a complex multi-dimensional phenomenon, operating at all levels from the intra- and interpersonal through to the global. Furthermore, the contrary and contesting visions of reality and possibility that ensue are themselves held within systems of power and relationship dynamics that often seek to reinforce the status quo. Hence conflicts and our experience of them can also be seen as being situated at different points along a number of axes: private–public; personal–communal; positive–pathological; low intensity–high intensity, etc. The dynamics shaping any particular conflict will depend, at least in part, on where it sits on one or more of these axes and on how they intersect. The attendant possibilities and appropriate responses will likewise vary and it can thus sometimes be helpful to add axes of response to our think-ing too: resolve–resist; transcend–transform, etc.

But though useful, this framework is also insufficient. Rather than being static phenomena, conflicts are dynamic, evolving systems and hence there is also an energy component which needs to be considered as we try to understand the economy of any given conflict: what drivers or pump primers are at work; where is energy being directed, trapped, wasted or consumed? Within any closed system, energy cannot be made or destroyed – it can only be transformed from one form into another. In many conflict situations (including internal ones), there is a tendency for us to become stuck as we adopt positions which slowly become entrenched, or as we allow ourselves to be hemmed in by particular narratives or understandings (of which we may not even be aware) which restrict our choices for creative action. In such situations, energy that could be used in positive ways is directed instead towards defensive manoeuvres and becomes locked up in reinforced stories, iden-tities, prejudices and patterns of behaviour, and thus no longer available to aid change. This raises questions as to where available energy within a conflict might be redirected; where trapped energy might be released and transformed into a more creative form; and where or how a closed conflict system might be opened up to allow the influx of new sources of energy in order to bring about change.

Thinking about a conflict system in terms of its energy can also provide us with another useful angle of insight – one which comes from complexity science. All systems – from weather to conflict – exhibit characteristic behaviours or have particular states towards which they evolve, or to which they return after they have been disturbed – their asymptotic behav-iour or so-called 'attractors'. The term is slightly misleading since an 'attractor' does not imply or involve the use of force, it simply provides evidence of the way in which the overall organization of a system constrains the alternatives available to it. Attractors tend to be determined by multiple factors, with those specifically at work in conflict systems being of the kind outlined above. They are also typically what we might think of as 'lower energy states' – that is, they are patterns we tend towards because they require less emotional, psychological or physical energy to maintain (one of the reasons why it can be very hard to alter patterns of behaviour or thought). Attention to the energy lines in a system can thus also direct us towards the things in that system – narratives, attitudes, beliefs, etc. – that may need working at before change can occur ('energy input' can be a helpful thought here). Understanding the factors which shape these various attractors in a conflict system can also help us better understand the shapes the system might take and the patterns of behaviour exhibited by those within it, particularly in respect to perceived threats of various kinds. It is beyond the scope of this essay to go into this further but Peter Coleman's recently published book *The Way Out*, which examines conflict in the light of insights from complexity theory, is a rich repository of further insights and helpful examples.[3]

Any spirituality of conflict needs to be attentive to these very different complexities and be able to furnish us with a range of appropriate tools for recognizing, exploring and engaging with them. One core aim of the project has thus been to offer a variety of lenses and strategies for use in the two-way process of 'reading the gospel texts through the lens of conflict and reading conflict through the lens of the gospel texts'. Sunday by Sunday and season by season, the set gospel readings are explored by different writers for dynamics relevant to conflict. The insights revealed by the text are then offered as lenses through which we can re-examine the everyday conflicts we each face in contemporary life – whether those be private or public, small scale or systemic, creative or destructive. However, this is only part of the story, since alongside the wisdom they offer us on human behaviour, the gospel texts also continuously challenge us with the vision of life as God intends – the full, flourishing, abundant life of which Jesus speaks and which his own life demonstrates; a life informed by the justice, peace and love which are the hallmarks of God's kingdom.

Thus, a second aim of the project has also been to explore how this vision speaks to the matter of conflict at every level from the personal to the systemic and of the contrast between this and the *shālômic* life offered through the kingdom. In this way we hope that the rich wisdom which the texts have to offer about human being and divine intention can inform our perceptions, praxis and prayer as we grapple with this most ubiquitous of experiences.

This brings us back to the question of whether and how such an endeavour can be thought of as 'spiritual' or in terms of 'a spirituality' of conflict. Although 'spiritual/spirituality' are widely used terms – often as a contrast to religion/religious ('spiritual but not religious') – precise meanings can be somewhat difficult to pin down, with definitions and usage varying. Generally speaking, the word 'spirituality' functions as an umbrella term, covering a constellation of themes by which we seek to give structure and assign meaning to our life-worlds: identity, interconnectedness, morality, ultimacy, transcendence, etc. As with other contexts, Christianity has its own particular ways of nuancing these which reflect its evolving narratives and self-understandings. But since these too are varied, even arriving at an agreed Christian understanding of spirituality can be far from straightforward! However, the words – which are derived from the Latin words *spiritus* and *spiritualitas* and thus the Greek words *pneuma* and *pneumatikos* of which these are the translations – and the way they functioned in the earliest Christian communities, can provide helpful orientation points.

The original Greek words are closely connected with the ancient Hebrew word *ruach*, relating to the movement of air. Occurring across the whole historical sweep of the Hebrew scriptures and variously translated breath, air, wind and spirit, the term is strongly connected with life and with various symbols of Yahweh's creative and renewing activity. That sense of animating power was carried forward by the New Testament authors and conjoined with the experiences of the nascent Christian community of the Holy Spirit as God's gift to them: the Advocate promised by Jesus who comforted, helped, reminded and continued to teach them (John 14.16–17, 26) as they strove to bring their lives into conformity with Christ and with the vision and values of a kingdom where all could find their place and flourish as God intended. Thus, rather than a realm of separate, inward, rarefied experience, spirituality – the experience of the workings of the Holy Spirit – was an integral part of routine individual and communal life. It was something that helped people orientate themselves to the purposes of God and navigate life in ways which were consonant with these; that encouraged them to recall and grow into the teachings of Jesus; and that supported them in the work of developing and sustaining hospitable relationships and of repairing them when they inevitably broke down. This perception of spirituality as something which both *animates* and *integrates* provides a useful anchor point as we try to tease out what a specific spirituality of conflict might entail.

The first element points towards it being something which will help us to breathe both *in* and *into* our understandings of conflict. Thinking about breath and breathing, particularly the physicality of it, opens up a number of fruitful avenues to explore here. The basic mechanics of breathing itself speak of a spirituality of conflict as being one that involves opening up and expanding spaces, drawing in fresh insights or energy, helping to remove potentially toxic ideas or imagery, etc. The role of breath in speaking or making music points us towards a spirituality which will help us to find our own voice, to articulate ideas and understandings, or to speak out against oppressive systems, to find clearer, more imaginative, or more generous ways to talk with one another. The experience of attention to our own breathing can direct us to the role of such a spirituality in being able to centre or steady us in difficult situations, or to locate us in the realities of our own embodied existence. These can then also alert us to ways in which the gospel texts might have wisdom from which we can learn: where are there spaces in a story, how are they changed by what people do and what are the outcomes? Where is the energy in a story directed? What gives life/causes death to any interactions or intentions? What speech acts occur, what is the purpose of the speaker and what happens as a result? Is there anything in the text which acts as a stabilizing/anchoring/sheltering point to those involved? A spirituality of conflict will be one which helps us to see and explore these possibilities in the text and bring the resulting insights into conversation with our own experiences of conflict.

The second element introduces a further important dimension – namely, that it will also be one which helps us to develop and integrate our understandings of different aspects of conflict in various ways. Conflict is at its heart an issue of relational disruption of some kind, with ourselves or with others – from individuals through to groups and nations, the wider created order and ultimately God. But, as we have already noted, conflicts are also complex entities involving many different elements, only some of which we may be aware of at times. Any spirituality of conflict will therefore need to be one that enables us to better understand the webs of history, narrative, identity, etc., within which our experiences of these relational disruptions are woven, and how these interconnect with and influence each other. It will also be one that helps us to see and explore our own particular perceptions of such things, particularly where those may be opaque to us.

Alongside this, though, any such spirituality also has an important role in helping us to look at all of these different elements in light of the vision of the kingdom of God set out by Jesus, showing up what might need to be affirmed and strengthened, challenged or changed. This vision is captured in the iridescent concept of *shālôm* – a word which, like *ruach*, appears across the whole canon of the Hebrew scriptures and which is also strongly associated with God, in this instance with God's love, faithfulness and righteousness. Often simply translated 'peace', the idea has a richness and multidimensionality transcending any narrow legal sense of order and encompassing the wholeness, healing, well-being and flourishing of all. Seen as a divine gift – something built into the very fabric of a universe from which God had driven back chaos and filled with righteousness, justice and merciful love – *shālôm* was not a private inner state but something that had to be actualized in individual, communal and national life. It thus was, and remains, in the words of moral theologian Enda McDonagh, 'at once gift and task'.[4] A spirituality that helps us to better understand and engage with a complexity that can often impede and disrupt *shālôm*, while also being sometimes integral to its development, is thus an important tool for use in this task.

This leads us finally to an account of how task and tool have been brought together in the current project. The gospel texts address conflict about all sorts of different things – identity, power, exclusion, holiness, money, etc. – and in many different ways. On some occasions conflict is even introduced or escalated by Jesus himself. There are stories of conflicts between individuals, as, for example, when the disciples argue about greatness in Mark 9 or get angry with James and John in Matthew 20; between people and authorities or systems such as when Jesus overturns the tables in John 2; or located in clashes between different expectations or understandings as in the exchanges between Peter and Jesus in Mark 8. Conflicts can also be lurking in the background of a story, sometimes in plain sight: Luke sets the birth of Jesus amid a census which was essentially a means of enabling a controlling foreign power to extract taxes from a subjugated people. Sometimes the possibility is raised more obliquely: is the hurried nature of Mary's journey to see Elizabeth in Luke 2 driven by excitement or, as Elisabeth Schüssler Fiorenza has suggested,[5] because of the dangers for a young woman of travelling in occupied territory? In many passages, conflict may seem to be entirely absent: what could we possibly draw, for example, from the Lucan text traditionally set for the naming of Jesus, with its joyous shepherds, thoughtful Mary and simple statement of bald facts around the actual naming? However, when we start to dig into these texts, especially when we look at them through different lenses, we can begin to see other things which underpin the surface layers, or possibilities beyond the ostensive meanings we habitually ascribe to them: the beauty and glory of the gospel texts is that their richly textured depths can neither be exhausted by a single reading nor contained and constrained within any one particular interpretive framework. Instead, the stories they contain, the larger narratives of which these are part, and the way the texts themselves have been put together, offer a rich repository of wisdom which transcends both the historical or cultural specificities which might have been the original authorial intent, or ones which have subsequently been imparted to them by particular theologies. Similarly, the parables of Jesus are rarely simple allegories to be decoded, or a didactic way of making moral points; rather, just as they were when delivered by Jesus, they are interactive devices for stimulating engagement and drawing out questions which lead to critical reflection on our ways of being and doing.[6] The gospel texts – as they have done throughout their history – always invite us into conversation and have a generous hospitality which makes space for our questions and probings.

Unfortunately, however, there are various things that can prevent these conversations from realizing their full potential – or sometimes from even getting started at all. The way we have been taught to receive or understand certain passages within wider theological narratives – such as those around sin and salvation for example, the thematic titles given to sections of the gospels in different translations, sometimes even the way the lectionary itself functions in linking passages – can all be impediments to this kind of reading: we can associate passages so strongly with particular themes (for example, the second coming) that it can sometimes be difficult to notice what other issues they might also be able to speak to, or what other wisdoms they might be offering us. There can also be a tendency with certain passages, especially ones where the story also occupies an important place in a larger theological narrative, to collapse the whole passage into its end point and in so doing to pay insufficient attention to what actually happens along the way. A good example here would be Luke's story of the Annunciation: almost as soon as we hear 'in the sixth month' we mentally leap to 'let it be with me according to your word'. But in between those points in the text, there is a whole process of reflection, internal debate and external interrogation. Far from being the foregone conclusion we assume (because we know the end of the story), what Luke is actually showing us is a journey which offers a range of rich and relevant insights. Any of these issues can leave us in danger of being like the prospector described by Marcel – overlooking, ignoring or discarding anything in a text that doesn't quite chime with our global reading or pre-determined end point.

In light of the first part of the project's remit ('reading the gospel texts through the lens of conflict'), the aim in these reflections has thus been to invite and encourage what we might call – again following Marcel's thought – an alternative hermeneutic of exploration. This is one which, rather than allowing a presumed 'meaning of the text' to dictate the way we read it, encourages us instead to approach the passage with an openness to receive and be enriched by any of the many different gifts it may contain, particularly as these can contribute to our understanding of conflict. The reflections seek to facilitate this exploration in a variety of ways: sometimes by directing our gaze to different spaces and gaps in the texts from those we normally focus on, or by marking out particular stopping points in a narrative from which to pause and survey the scene; at other times by offering different lenses through which to read the text, or by suggesting alternative sight lines to try out as ways of looking at it.

The reflections may focus on the material in the text itself, or on the way it fits in with larger themes, but also on the way we actually read it, and the kind of lenses with which we are (perhaps unknowingly) doing this. In keeping with the project's second remit ('reading conflict through the lens of the gospel texts'), suggestions are also offered as to how we can then take these 'gratuitous gifts' offered by the text and use them as lenses through which to read and examine the conflicts that affect us. Since the writers in the project come from a variety of backgrounds and experiences, each approaches the task from different starting points and with different tools and the result is a rich and varied mixture of reflections. These are written in different styles and with different emphases but all aim to encourage us to engage with the texts in ways which not only help us to deepen our understanding of conflict, but also to respond to conflicts in more informed ways which allow new creative possibilities to emerge.

Thus, there is a real sense in which a spirituality of conflict *is* a spirituality of peace and reconciliation, albeit one that approaches these from a rather different starting point. Peace – in all its *shālômic* glory – is indeed the message at the heart of the Gospel but, in the words of Brendan McAllister, a veteran of the Northern Ireland peace process, 'the work of peace begins within the work of conflict'.[7] And such work is not just for those who are professional mediators, it is a task to which the Gospel calls each one of us – and it is a task which, crucially, begins with ourselves.

It is in support of this task that the Spirituality of Conflict resource is offered as a contribution.

God of carefully chosen words,
God of unfinished truth telling:
be with us
as we do the work
of talking with ourselves.
Before we go out
to address a conflict
or offer peace,
or seek reconciliation,
may we engage
in an inner conversation
of challenge and honesty,
deep in a private humanity
we discover we share.
Amen.[8]

Notes

1 Pádraig Ó Tuama, unpublished.

2 Gabriel Marcel, *The Existential Background of Human Dignity* (Cambridge, MA: Harvard University Press, 1963), p. 8.

3 Peter T. Coleman, *The Way Out: How to Overcome Toxic Polarization* (New York: Columbia University Press, 2021).

4 Enda McDonagh, 'Peace Makers or Justice Seekers' in *Born Free and Equal, Pax Christi and Human Rights* (Brussels: Pax Christi International, 1990).

5 Elisabeth Schüssler Fiorenza, *Jesus: Miriam's Child, Sophia's Prophet* (London: Continuum, 1994).

6 John Dominic Crossan, *The Power of Parable* (London: SPCK, 2012).

7 Brendan McAllister, 'On Peace and the Spaces Between the Words' in *Think Peace, Essays for an Age of Disorder* (Carnegie, 2014), p. 53.

8 Alex Wimberly © 2021 The Corrymeela Community, used with permission.

Introducing the Selections
in this Volume

Pat Bennett

The Spirituality of Conflict project is now in its second passage through the three years of the lectionary cycle. When the project began in 2016, one of our general principles was to avoid tying the weekly reflections to specific national or international events current at the time of writing. However, given the world-changing nature of the Covid-19 pandemic, this no longer felt appropriate and hence more recently written reflections do reference this, especially given the way it has exposed or heightened many of the dynamics and patterns which instigate or perpetuate conflict, at individual, community and national levels.

While many reflections address underlying ubiquitous elements of conflict, some focus more on specific areas of conflict such as climate justice, church conflict or sectarianism. Others look at how conflict disrupts our life-worlds or at what practices can sustain, shelter or nurture us as we engage with this disruption. Pieces are written with a view to being accessible and helpful, both for those engaging with them as part of a personal journey and those preparing sermons or services based around the lectionary gospel readings.

As this volume is an introduction to the project, the aim has also been to highlight and illustrate the different possibilities sketched out in the introductions as to how to bring a conflict lens to the texts and then use their wisdom to examine our own conflict experiences. As part of this, especially given the wide variety of authorial backgrounds and styles, we also wished to include contributions from all the writers. However, since seasonal 'blocks' have tended to be assigned to a single author, such representation is inevitably unequal in a volume of this nature. For this reason, there are also three pieces which, strictly speaking, fall outside of the designated seasons but which have been included so that the voices of all the core contributors to the project could be represented.

Based on the gospel texts from the Revised Common Lectionary (and the NRSV translation), a reflection is provided for each of the three years of the cycle for the Sundays in Advent and Lent; for Ash Wednesday and the weekdays in Holy Week; for the festivals of the Nativity, the Resurrection of the Lord and the Holy Name of Jesus; and for Easter Evening and Easter 2. Where an identical text occurs across all three years, there is a selection of reflections from different perspectives. Within each section, reflections are grouped by lectionary year rather than by the specific Sundays within the season.

Sometimes writers have chosen to explore the seasonal readings from the perspective of a particular theme or motif which they follow across all the gospel texts, allowing for more sustained attention to a specific area. Hence, for each season, the reflections for one of the years of the cycle are offered in the form of a thematic 'set', often with slightly longer reflections: the Advent/Christmas readings for Year B consider the nature of looking; for Lent in Year B they explore the conversations and tensions between private and public as seen in the life of Jesus; and for Holy Week the focus is on the different types of spaces occupied by people in the passion and resurrection narratives.

Each piece includes an introduction to the text, often with suggestions for preparation, a reflection, some possibilities for framing a response and a prayer based on these. All pieces have previously appeared – sometimes in a slightly longer form – on the Spirituality of Conflict website (www.spiritualityofconflict. com). All pieces are indexed by author, text and themes.

Copyright for pieces remains with the individual authors unless otherwise indicated.

Reflections for the
Season of Advent and
the Nativity of the Lord

Advent Year A

Advent Sunday – Matthew 24.36–44

Pat Bennett

Introduction

Themes of anticipation, preparation and recognition run through all the gospel readings to which we traditionally turn our attention during the season of Advent. They are also always coupled with the imperative for a response and accounts of the different forms this might take. In the readings we follow this Advent, Matthew chooses to emphasize preparation and response – but at various points he also weaves different paradoxes into his narrative which throw into sharp relief the true nature of both king and kingdom whose coming we look for in this season. Today's reading certainly introduces various questions about anticipation and preparation but it also points us, less directly, towards a particular dynamic which may come into play when hopes and expectations are disappointed and when what we long for seems deliberately thwarted by the actions of others. As we begin our journey through the three-year lectionary cycle, reading conflict through the lens of the gospels, this seems a very appropriate place to begin.

Preparation

Think about an event which you were eagerly anticipating but which did not turn out as you expected. What emotions were predominant? How do those emotions influence your recollections? How did they affect your responses to the situation at the time?

Comment

Traditionally reflections on this text tend to focus on the nature of awareness and watchfulness and the importance of appropriate preparation; or perhaps on how we can hold the balance between being prepared for a future event and 'getting on with other things' while we wait for it. However, the reading also points us towards a huge paradox – albeit not one which Matthew intentionally introduces. This paradox is one which is built into the tonal progression of his gospel itself: a narrative whose opening announces a great theology of *inclusion* – outsiders, the questionable and the downright scandalous are key figures in the genealogy of Jesus – progresses towards one in which the leitmotif becomes one of *exclusivity*. Similarly, the warm, expansive and generous feel contained in the gospel's first discourse – the famous 'Sermon on the Mount' – stands in stark contrast to its final discourse, from which today's passage comes, with its woes, vituperative language and warnings of apocalyptic judgement and destruction.

If we look at the audiences to which the five discourses are addressed we can trace out what seems to be a parallel shift: the Sermon on the Mount (Matt. 5.1—7.29) is offered to all; the second discourse (10.5–42) is given to the disciples and initiates the proclamation and establishment of the kingdom; the parables of the third (13.1–52) begin to articulate a narrative of inclusion/exclusion – those who do and don't belong to that kingdom (and again there is a shift away from the crowds to the disciples); the fourth discourse (18.1–35) seems to be exclusively directed towards the nascent kingdom community, with instructions as to how to remain within it; and the final discourse (24.1; 25.46), with its strong and difficult language, is directed against its enemies, those who are seen as opposing it.

What we get is a sense of escalating conflict underpinning and shaping the purpose of Matthew's narrative. If we look at this in its historical context we can perhaps begin to see where this might be coming from. Matthew's Gospel was written primarily for Jewish Christians and scholarly opinion dates it, for various reasons, as some time after the destruction of the temple in AD 70. This cataclysmic event meant that Judaism could no longer be a temple-centred, sacrificially enacted religion and had to find a new form. However – as is clear from the course of history – it did not find that shape through the newly established and developing vision of the kingdom of God articulated by Jesus. So it may well be that what we see reflected in the changing keys of Matthew's narrative is a reflection of the author's own disappointed hopes and his frustration and anger that something which had never been intended as an alternative to Judaism, or to exclude its adherents, had been forced into a position of conflict with it.

The chilling narrowing of this gospel's emotional key from generosity to condemnation, and the changing narrative dynamic from openness to exclusion, point us towards what can happen if we let the hurt, anger, or frustration of disappointed hopes or unrealized expectations take control of our outlook: hospitality changes into hostility; generosity is replaced by judgement; and others become enemies to be resisted rather than guests to be welcomed. It alerts us to the fact that one of the key dynamics in situations of conflict can be a progressive narrowing – in various different ways – of the spaces we inhabit, and thus a restriction of the degrees of freedom within which we can operate. The end result is to close down the possibilities for creative response and drive us deeper into our own trenches.

Response

Reflect on a situation – either personal or related to work or church – where your attitude towards another person or group has changed. What direction has that change been in? See if you can trace that trajectory, identifying any markers of the kind discussed above and reflecting on what these tell you about this particular relational journey. Are there things you would or could change in this instance, or if you encounter a similar situation again?

Prayer

A prayer of confession

Leader: Jesus our brother
You call us to a daily journey
of ongoing conversion
in our thinking, our loving and our living ...

All: We recognize and confess those times
when fear and anxiety
have deafened us to your call
and imprisoned us in a barren place.

silence

Leader: Jesus, forgive us
All: Forgive us and free us.

We recognize and confess those times
when anger and bitterness
have deafened us to your call
and imprisoned us in a barren place.

silence

Leader: Jesus, forgive us
All: Forgive us and free us.

We recognize and confess those times
when broken relationships and dreams
have deafened us to your call
and imprisoned us in a barren place.

silence

Leader: Jesus, forgive us
All: Forgive us and free us.

Leader: It is for freedom that Christ has set us free –
go and live out the freedom of God!

Advent 2 – Matthew 3.1–12

Janet Foggie

Introduction

John the Baptist was a forager and believer in a natural life-style. The protest elements of his ministry were wearing clothes of leather and eating foraged food, locusts and wild honey. He might fit well today with those who practise 'die-ins', lying on the road to prevent fossil fuels being burned, or who inhabit trees to prevent road or runway construction. He was a pro-tester, a voice shouting in the wilds. Jesus was the prophet, the son of God, the man with the radical message. The protester John grabbed attention, Jesus followed and hammered home his gospel: good news for some, and the end of entitlement and entrenched power for others. Sometimes conflict or dissonance is a necessary precursor to change.

Comment

If we take the role of protester and prophet for our reflection this week then it might be illustrative to look at the impact of the Youth Climate Strikes and the work of Greta Thunberg who addressed the United Nations on 23 September 2019. Just as with John and the Pharisees and Sadducees, the protesters have roundly criticized the adult leaders of their communities. Greta Thunberg said, 'How dare you!' with her whole person filled with emotion as she described the leaders of the world as obsessed with money and careless of the future of the planet. Those leaders, and many who subscribe to their values, have not been slow to excoriate her and she has faced a barrage of insults on social media and in mainstream media. But the powerful message she brings has the force of truth: the polar regions have a crisis we cannot control; the Amazon is burning; the people who live by the Zambezi fear they will never see its annual floods again in their lifetime.

The radical protester who has a plant-based diet, or who only eats foraged foods, or sustainably raised meat, or whatever the protest is, is a necessary part of a society facing a crisis. We need to see extremes in order to get the main body of opinion to shift. In this current case, we have known the facts of climate change since I was Greta's age, more than a quarter of a century ago. What we have been unable to do is to get the environmental science to influence the majority of ordinary citizens. In all those years, even knowing what I know, I have bought and sold cars, taken flying for granted and only made those changes which it was easy to make.

John uses the analogy of a tree that needs to be cut down. The petrol-based economy is literally cutting down trees that bear good fruit. We want to be able to clear our own consciences, and so going on a litter pick might salve the soul but it doesn't cancel the impact of commuting, using a petrol car for short urban journeys, buying single-use plastic or flying for holidays or work. We also like to point to the complexity of the problems in order to excuse ourselves from doing the little we can. Just because a vegan burger might contain imported soya from more than one country doesn't excuse the purchasing of junk food with intensively farmed and processed beef (which is probably fed the same imported soya). Both the soya and the beef need to be more sustainably farmed and eaten more locally.

Equally, the human justice required of our world leaders is for them to ensure that the world's wealth, food, health resources, and even those few oil-based products we really do need and can afford to keep, are more fairly redistributed. A good example is the need for accessible and widely used public transport as a viable option for the majority of urban journeys. Many people cite the inadequacy of public transport as a reason for taking the car on an urban journey. These sort of 'helpless cycles' are really easy excuses for not mobilizing a bigger social change. If we improve public transport, we also need to incentivize the use of it in order to ensure cars are not being used in urban areas where the effects of the air pollution are greatest.

If we want to hear the voice of John the Baptist today, we need look no further than Greta Thunberg. The question for us, as it was in Jesus' day, is: are we wheat to be gathered into the granary, caring about our world neighbours; or are we chaff to be thrown into the global winnowing fire?

Response

Consider any actions you can take to reduce your CO_2 emissions. These might be turning down your thermostat, car sharing, using public transport, taking a 'no-fly' holiday.

Alternatively, think about the similarities between Greta Thunberg and John the Baptist. What can you do to add your voice to the prophetic call to action to slow the climate crisis? Is speaking out enough? What other actions could you take?

Prayer

God of eternity, we come before you today
sorry for all those children who could turn to us and say,
'You have stolen my dreams and my childhood.'
For children facing an uncertain world due to climate crisis,
and our part in burning the fossil fuels of our planet.
We are sorry for the wrong we have done to the children
whose future we have gobbled up in shopping,
and using the earth's resources.
We hear the children saying, 'How dare you!'
And we are sorry
Sorry to the pit of our stomachs
Sorry to the bottom of our hearts.
Forgive us, gracious God,
and let that forgiveness be neither easy nor quickly forgotten.

Silence

We pray to you, our God who forgives before we ask,
however little we deserve it.
As we step towards you to receive that forgiveness
so may we be enabled to live more humbly,
consume less and grow more like Jesus every day.
Amen.

Advent 3 – Matthew 11.2–11

Janet Foggie

Introduction

At Christmas time, a lot of people, for whom it isn't a usual part of their week, temporarily 'notice' Christians and Christianity more. Sometimes this leads to an over-sentimentalizing of religion, but also sometimes to a criticism of 'religious people'. Jesus questions the expectations that people had of John, and similarly we too need to query our own expectations.

The conflict this week is between the pious, the holy, the prophet trying to live a better life, and those whom they hope to inspire yet often alienate instead. The challenge of this week is not to obsess about the people who find us difficult but rather to think of the places where we ourselves are challenged.

Comment

One of the most interesting features of this passage is that the supposedly unshakable John the Baptist is sending his disciples to query whether Jesus is 'the one' or whether they are to wait for 'another'. It isn't often we get to see the insecurities of a prophet. Last week in the desert, proud and vocal, John had seemingly unmovable faith in Jesus as the Messiah. This week, in prison and alone, he isn't so sure. Jesus reassures his imprisoned friend. He talks of the things God does to bring in his kingdom: the blind are healed, the lame walk, the poor receive good news ... Jesus does not refer to himself, his preaching or his authority, but instead reassures John, through his disciples, by listing the effects of the kingdom, a ministry of praxis, or practical activity.

Last week we compared the Baptist to Greta Thunberg and considered her prophetic voice in a world of climate crisis. We thought about the need to hear her words not just as a rousing speech but as a call to personal action. Jesus adds to his reassurance to John the sentence, 'And blessed is anyone who takes no offense at me.' People had taken offence at John's message and indeed had imprisoned him; people would take offence at Jesus and his ministry of healing or his focus on the poor. In the same way, a great many people, from celebrities to world leaders to ordinary folks, have taken offence at the words of Greta Thunberg. Many of the insults hurled at her are too offensive to repeat here.

However, taking offence can be an all-too-easy escape from the challenge of mending our behaviour and while Christmas is often a time of giving to foodbanks, homeless charities and charities abroad, it is also a time when we spend money with very different priorities from our normal weekly shop.

We need to consider, this Advent, the shocking level of single-use expenditure which we simply excuse for ourselves. Whether it is crackers, or plastic decorations, or extra lights. We buy novelty toys and novelty socks, Christmas-themed jumpers, headbands, earrings ... The list can go on and it is very hard to reverse this trend and buy a few gifts that will last longer. And the choices are not always straightforward: Christmas tree growers are one of the largest users of the weed-killer glyphosate because they want to keep weeds down among the growing trees. A plastic Christmas tree, if re-used many times, might be a more environmentally friendly option, or a tree which was organically grown.

And then, of course, we have that natural reaction to take offence at the prophets, those annoying 'holier than thou' people who preach on about such things or give lentils and jute as gifts. And here is the nub of the issue: the offence taken also includes unacknowledged guilt. If we can't face the guilt, we cannot accept our part in the climate crisis, and we cannot unlock our habits and make ourselves open to change.

Yet Jesus said, 'Blessed is anyone who takes no offense at me.' This lays down a strong challenge: to accept the guilt of only being able to do so much and the simultaneous challenge to do more. This is the clarion call this Advent.

Response

What can you do personally to have a more environmentally friendly Christmas? Can you take public transport when visiting family? Can you source an organic Christmas tree or reuse an old one? Can you have a 'shop-free' Advent?

Think about people who annoy you: are there people who, even just by being themselves, seem to threaten or question your lifestyle or habits? What is it about their lifestyle or views you find challenging? Are they different from you in diet, or political beliefs or religion? Can you get together with someone who is really different in views or background and have a good conversation about that difference?

Prayer

Offensive God,
We bring before you the offence we take.
The times we find others to be too holy, too pious, too
  politically correct.
The times we find others too traditional, too inflexible, too
  set in their ways.
When our sin is to judge others
as unacceptable, impossible to stomach, preachy or
  hypocritical ...
Forgive us our judgemental days.
Forgive us for taking offence.
Forgive us for harsh words or cruel jokes.
Enable us to see the good in the good efforts of others.
Widen our eyes to a better world.
Help us find the courage to speak our own views with reason.
And when we need to change our views for the better,
do not let our naturally offended excuses put us off.
Amen.

Advent 4 – Matthew 1.18–25

Pat Bennett

Introduction

Today we encounter the fourth and final paradox which the gospel readings for this Advent bring before us. The Infancy narratives of Matthew's Gospel – in contrast to those of Luke – say very little about the birth of Jesus per se. Instead, the writer concentrates on the reactions of two men – one before and one after – to the news of the event. We will be considering Herod's response during Epiphany, but today the focus is on that of Joseph. By framing the preceding lineage of Jesus in terms of fatherhood (in contrast to the Lucan stress of sonship), Matthew has already prepared us for his account of the way in which the actions of Joseph – by confounding the expectations of the social and religious conventions of his time – pave the way for the purposes of God to unfold in the world.

Comment

Matthew tells us nothing about Joseph's immediate reactions to the discovery of Mary's pregnancy, but it is not hard to imagine his confusion and the emotions of anger and distress which would have been part of the first, visceral response to such a staggering piece of news.

Marriages in antiquity were made between extended families, not individuals, and the process of dis-embedding a young woman from her father's family and embedding her in that of her new husband involved the whole community and touched deeply on the honour of both families involved. Virginity was a *sine qua non* and thus its loss brought shame upon the woman's entire paternal family. In the case of Mary, that the apparent loss occurred during the period of betrothal was doubly shameful because of the significance of this period in the Jewish understanding of the marriage process.

This involved two distinct steps: *kiddushin* – the setting apart of a particular woman for a particular man, and *nisu'in* – the formal finalization of the marriage contract. At the time of Jesus' birth, these were separated by a significant period of time. *Kiddushin*, commonly translated 'betrothal', actually made the bride and groom a fully fledged husband and wife both spiritually and legally; thus, even if they did not complete the *nisu'in*, a *get* (Jewish divorce) was still required to end the contract.

However, it was only after the completion of the *nisu'in* ceremony that the couple were allowed to live together and engage in sexual relations. The period of betrothal was considered to be a time in which the foundations for the vital spiritual connection between husband and wife could be laid (*kiddushin* is also used in Hosea 2.19, 20 to designate the relationship between God and his people). Its importance is attested to by both the harsh punishment laid down in Deuteronomy for its violation, and the declaration in the Mishna (the first major written redaction of the oral Torah) that adultery during the betrothal period was more serious than adultery after marriage.

When set against this twin sociological and religious backdrop, the extraordinary and paradoxical nature of Joseph's actions can be fully appreciated. Deuteronomy 22.20–21 sets out the chilling punishment for women in Mary's situation. However, even before his dream Joseph displays a willingness to act outside expectations of what constitutes the normal, appropriate response in such a situation. The Greek verbs used in verses 19 and 20 to describe how he reached this initial plan of action are revealing. The first – *boulomai* ('planned')[1] – carries the implication of an actively willed choice; the second – *enthumeomai* ('resolved')[2] – means to reflect on or to ponder. In other words, this is a response which has been carefully thought through and deliberately chosen; and that choice is to find an alternative way to preserve the honour of his and Mary's families and the life of Mary and her unborn child.

This involved following (even in the absence of evidence) the direction in the accompanying Targum (an ancient Aramaic interpretive commentary on the Torah) which allowed for divorce rather than death under the very specific circumstance of rape out in the fields where help could not be summoned by the woman.

Interestingly, *enthumeomai* carries a dual meaning – it can also suggest becoming angry, something which heightens the drama of what Joseph ultimately chooses to do. So then we can perhaps imagine Joseph lying in bed – not tossing and turning before falling into a fevered sleep, but instead turning everything over and over in his mind and gradually reaching a place where the initial incredulity and anger no longer drives his response; a place where he is able to reflect on and actively choose another course of action. Perhaps it was the fact that he had already started on the pathway of seeking a less destructive and more generous response than that dictated by social and religious convention that subsequently enabled him to take the even more confounding route suggested through his dream of marrying Mary and himself assuming the responsibility of fatherhood for Jesus.

Cognitive neuroscience tells us that, whatever we might like to think, there is no such thing as a 'purely rational' decision: our first response to any situation – regardless of whether or not we are cognizant of it – is always rooted in the emotions. However, the story of Joseph shows that these initial – and perfectly natural – responses do not have to be what dictate our subsequent actions. Once again then, we have an example of how a willingness to step back from reflex responses and move outside our frameworks of understanding – whether these be connected to presuppositions about privilege, specific understandings and expectations about events or what constitutes a reasonable or legitimate way of behaving – opens up the possibility of developing richer understandings and more creative responses in the face of challenges. However, as our Advent readings have also indicated, this is not necessarily an easy path – and indeed is often a costly route to follow.

Response

Recall a time when a piece of news you received provoked a strong emotional reaction (positive or negative). Reflect on the extent to which your initial emotional responses determined your subsequent behaviour. How can we develop a practice that allows us to experience and own the inevitable (and perfectly natural) emotional responses which we have at certain moments but prevents these from dictating our subsequent reactions and actions in ways which may be unhelpful or destructive? What tools or skills might help us with this?

Prayer

May the peace of God –
the demanding peace of emotional engagement
the dangerous peace of imaginative action
the dynamic peace of Holy Dreaming –
fill your hearts with joy,
your lives with courage,
and your world with change.
Amen.

Notes

1 W. E. Vine, *Expository Dictionary of New Testament Words* (London: Oliphant, 1978), vol. I, p. 299.
2 Vine, *Expository Dictionary*, vol. IV, p. 128.

Advent Year B –
'Looking and Seeing'

The reflections for Advent Year B form a thematic set which also includes a reflection for Christmas (Proper 1 and Proper 2).

Introduction to the Set

Pat Bennett

Advent, the season of waiting, is also a time of watching – of looking and attending – and the Advent readings for Year B all tell us something about aspects of this very human activity. The questions they point us toward and which weave back and forth through the texts – How do we look? Where are we looking? What or who are we looking at? Why are we looking? What do we do with our seeing? – are all pertinent ones for us to consider in the context of developing a spirituality of conflict. They are also very apposite at this moment in time when the Covid-19 pandemic and significant political upheavals around the globe have not only exposed and heightened various conflicts but also given rise to widespread uncertainties and anxieties: never has the question 'What is left of the night?' – asked of the watchman in Isaiah 21 – seemed more pressing; never has the ambiguous reply of 'Morning is coming, but also the night' seemed more resonant.

Each reflection is followed by a series of questions for consideration – perhaps with reference to a specific conflict situation, perhaps with respect to things that are currently happening in public life, or perhaps more generally as a way of reflecting on our ongoing journey into God. The aim of these is not to provide rods with which to punish ourselves, but to help us examine and improve our practice. Looking properly, seeing clearly, understanding deeply, are difficult skills which take a lifetime to acquire and hone – as the gospel stories, particularly those relating to the disciples, make abundantly clear.

Advent Sunday – Mark 13.24–37

'How are we looking?'

Pat Bennett

Introduction

For Year B, Mark takes over as our principal companion and guide. However, the journey commences not at the beginning of his gospel but with the so-called 'little apocalypse' which sits at the heart of his passion narrative. At first sight this might seem a strange starting point but in fact this passage, with its repeated emphasis on the nature and quality of our looking, is a perfect place to set out for a journey through a gospel in which seeing is a central theme. Given that our passage today is inextricably linked via its first line to the preceding verses, it makes sense to attend also to the opening of the chapter as we consider this key theme.

Preparation

Read the whole of Mark 13 (in several versions if possible) and make a list of any words or phrases that you feel have a connection with looking, paying attention or seeing. Note the 'feel' of each word/phrase and write your own definition for it.

Comment

Reading material from the apocalyptic genre, particularly if divorced from its historical and cultural contexts, can be problematical. However, if we take a step back from these distractions, this text also has some key things to say about the nature of looking. 'Seeing' is an important Marcan leitmotif – key moments in his narrative are bookended by, or hinge upon, stories and incidents connected with blindness, partial or distorted seeing and seeing properly. This is not just about physical seeing, it is about understanding what we see – and how we *look* is a key part of this. Today's gospel passage, and the preceding verses which set it up, reference seeing on 15 occasions, outlining different types and qualities of looking as they do so.

First, there is what we might designate as 'distracted looking'. It is an example of this that sets the whole chapter in motion and leads to the words of Jesus here. He and his disciples have been in the temple where he has been giving answers – sometimes difficult and puzzling answers – to questions about himself, taxes, resurrection, money and love. But as they leave the building the disciples have something of a 'squirrel moment': '"Look, Teacher, what large stones and what large buildings!"' Jesus uses exactly the same disjunctive participle (*ide* – 'behold!') in verse 21 to describe something that will happen in the times about which he is warning them: 'Look ... the Messiah!' 'Look – there he is!' There are things – they might even be or appear to be good things – that can cause us to take our eye off the ball, to draw our attention away from what matters. Various mechanics could lie at the root of this distraction – perhaps we struggle to cope with the implications, complications, complexity or enormity of what we are seeing; perhaps someone else wants to deflect us (for good or bad reasons) from looking at and thinking about something. Whatever the reason, the net result is that we stop attending and thus we may fail to see, to understand, something that is important.

Then there is what we might call 'deep looking'. Mark uses two different verbs for seeing – *horaō* and *blepō* – at different points in the passage. While both are connected with bodily vision, the latter 'indicates a greater vividness ... expressing a more intent earnest contemplation,' 'it especially stresses the thought of the person who sees'.[1] In verses 14 and 26, which use *horaō*, it seems that Jesus is simply describing what people will see at these apocalyptic moments. The verb mood indicates that these are statements of facts – indications of what could or might happen. Contrast this with the feel of verses 5, 9, 23 and 33 where Mark uses *blepō* and moreover always uses it in the imperative (command) form: 'beware/see to it'; 'beware/be on your guard'; 'be alert/take heed'; 'beware/take heed'. The urgency is clear and although sometimes the English slightly obscures it, Jesus is telling his disciples not just to observe or note superficially but to really look, to get beyond the immediate surface appearance of things. Such looking takes time and effort; it needs awareness of the conditioned nature of our looking – of the different narratives, prejudices and experiences which influence our seeing – and of how these might shape and possibly distort it.

The closing section adds two final verbs which the NRSV renders 'keep alert' (v. 33), 'be on the watch' (v. 34) and 'keep awake' (v. 35 and v. 37), but which the RSV uniformly translates with the more old-fashioned 'watch' – a word strongly associated with Advent. In fact, 'watch' gives a better idea of what is going on here since the Greek words convey much more than simply battling sleepiness. In verse 33, *agrypneō* expresses 'not mere wakefulness, but the "watchfulness" of those who are intent upon a thing',[2] that is, it carries a sense of a concentrated attention – perhaps like the watchmen on the city walls intently examining the sky for the first signs of dawn, or constantly scanning the horizon for signs of disturbance or danger. Similarly, the etymological roots of *grēgoreō* (verses 34, 35 and 36)[3] move it away from being merely the opposite of being asleep to a much more active sense of collecting one's faculties – gathering up scattered thoughts or unconscious attentions and knitting these together into a unified, purposeful attentiveness. The watchmen don't just scan – they evaluate the information their senses give them and use it to inform their judgements and actions.

Jesus seems to be pointing here towards something that we could usefully think of as 'collected looking'. This, like the work of the watchmen, involves a more wide-ranging, active type of attention, one which takes an overview of different elements and pulls them together into fuller, more textured assessments and understandings.

This passage thus leaves us with a variety of angles from which to interrogate the nature and quality of our own looking in different situations, both conflict-related and more generally, as we journey through Advent. Some possible questions are suggested below but you may well have others or different ways of framing them which are more helpful for you.

Response

- Are there areas where I am struggling to be attentive in my looking, or allowing others (for good or bad reasons) to distract me from it? What might be going on? Does it matter? Do I need to try and find a remedy? Is there someone who could help me with this?
- Am I looking/willing to look beyond the immediate surface of things when necessary? Am I sufficiently aware of the things which might be conditioning my seeing? Does it matter? Is it something I ought to/can do something about? Is there someone who could help me with this?
- Am I looking for different sorts of information, or bringing together different elements, when I try to understand complex situations, make evaluative judgements or decide on appropriate actions? Are there ways in which I could develop/deepen these skills? Is there someone who could help me with this?

Prayer

Jesus
even you needed
to sometimes look
more than once
or with deeper attention
in order to properly see and understand
what was happening around you.

In this season of watching
may we too
be steady
brave
and diligent
in the work of looking
that through seeing more clearly
and understanding more richly
we may recognize and nurture
the signs of your kingdom
and resist all that opposes
its flourishing life
or undermines
its generous love
Amen.

Notes

1 W. E. Vine, *Expository Dictionary of New Testament Words* (London: Oliphant, 1978), vol. I, p. 114.

2 Vine, *Expository Dictionary*, vol. VI, p. 201.

3 For more information on etymologies, see Strong's Greek Lexicon, www.biblestudytools.com/lexicons/greek.

Advent 2 – Mark 1.1–8

'Where are we looking?'

Pat Bennett

Introduction

Mark's account of Jesus starts in a very different way to that of his fellow evangelists: there are no genealogies, birth narratives or sweeping poetry. However, it does give us an early indication of something which will be a key theme in his gospel and it leads us to the second of our Advent questions about looking – that of 'Where?' What is the direction of our gaze?

Preparation

Find a famous image with which you are reasonably familiar. Spend some time looking at it but paying attention only to what is going on around the edges or in the less eye-catching parts. What do you notice? Does it change how you read or understand the image? In what way?

Alternatively, watch a few scenes from a movie you know well but, instead of looking at the central action, attend to what is happening out of centre shot or at the edges of the frame. Do you notice anything you haven't been aware of before? Does it add anything to, or change anything about, the way you see the scene or the bigger narrative? In what way?

Comment

We, of course, know who 'John the Baptizer' is – but imagine for a moment that we did not have the accounts of Luke and John to fill in the background information which Mark totally fails to provide. What we would then have is a smattering of prophetic allusions, an alien environment, an eccentric figure and a somewhat Delphic announcement! Not, perhaps, what we might expect for 'the beginning of the good news'. However, this is simply the first taste of the overthrow of expectations which permeates Mark's Gospel and it points us towards the second of our Advent 'looking' questions – that of 'Where?'

Mark often uses a repeated key word or phrase to mark the beginning and end of a section of the narrative and to indicate the purpose and focus of the intervening passage (a literary device known as *inclusio*). He does this on a large scale for his whole gospel in fact: the announcement here in verse 1, that it is about 'Jesus Christ, the Son of God', and its echo in the centurion's comment that, 'Truly, this man was God's Son' (15.39) underline that everything which Mark writes has the aim of helping his hearers (including us) see the hidden truth about Jesus. He wants them to look at Jesus properly – with the deep, collected looking we discussed last week – because only then will they understand who he is and what his Messiahship actually entails.

Today's passage raises the critical question, to which Mark repeatedly returns, of where we need to look if we want to see God and find his Messiah at work. Mark is not governed by our chapter/verse conventions (or liturgical seasons!), so our gospel reading is actually part of the longer section (vv. 1–15) which is bookended (in Mark's opening statement and his first recorded speech for Jesus) with a reference to *euangelion* – 'the good news'. Once again, the use of an *inclusio* alerts us to the fact that Mark is using this opening section to set out some important elements of this 'good news of Jesus Christ'. His use of prophetic fragments from Isaiah, Ezekiel and Malachi makes it clear that it is not 'the good news' itself which is unexpected – on the contrary this is what the Jewish people have long been anticipating in the light of God's past actions, as recorded in their sacred texts. What is strange and startling, however, is the location in which it is unfolding.

While the desert had a strong tradition as a place for encounter with the divine, expectations about the Messiah were of a triumphant figure who would destroy Israel's enemies and free and restore Jerusalem. So for Mark to situate 'the beginning' at a place on the margins, rather than in Jerusalem, the heart of the nation, is unexpected and disconcerting. Verse 5 further underscores this counterintuitive flow of movement – it was not just people from the countryside around who came to John, but people from Jerusalem, from the centre itself, who travelled to the rim to see what was happening. And although the baptism of Jesus himself is beyond our remit today, it's worth noting that this too, with its accompanying theophany, takes place at an edge (the Jordan was the boundary marker for the promised land). Moreover, Jesus – the locus of the ultimate revelation about God – must go even further into the wilderness to find its confirmation.

This removal of God from the centre to the margins occurs throughout Mark's Gospel and is one of his key points: the kingdom of God and its Messiah are consistently *not* where people are looking or expecting to find them. This is sometimes inextricably linked to the issue of what people are looking for – a question we will consider in Advent 3 – but the theme plays out in a variety of other ways too: Mark's Jesus is constantly to be found doing the work of the kingdom, not among the powerful and elite, but among those who are, for different reasons, on the edges. Furthermore, it is usually these characters at the margins, rather than those at the heart of religious or national identity, who recognize and acknowledge Jesus for what he is.

For Mark, seeing Jesus properly thus requires not only that we deepen and develop the quality of our looking, but also that we attend intentionally to the direction of our gaze: we need to be aware that sometimes we have to consciously de-centre this and start looking in other than what seem to us to be the obvious or the logical places. Mark ends his gospel by making the point explicitly: the original (shorter) ending details no encounters with the risen Jesus; instead, it describes the women going to the tomb to find and tend to Jesus' remains only to be told, 'You are looking for Jesus of Nazareth, who was crucified. He has been raised; he is not here … he is going ahead of you to Galilee.' Once again, and in more ways than one, says Mark, people were looking in the wrong place for God.

Today's gospel passage therefore gives us another angle from which to examine our looking in situations of conflict (and more generally) as we travel through the watching season of Advent: when we are trying to increase our understanding, or to find signs of hope, change, etc., where are we directing our gaze – and is this the right or the best place? Some possible questions for exploring this are suggested below.

Response

• To what extent do I think about where I am looking when I'm seeking for answers, deeper understandings, solutions, possibilities of change, etc.? Does this matter? What things might help me to be more consciously attentive to this aspect of my practice of looking?

• What sort of things influence where I direct my gaze? Have I missed or misread something because I've been looking in the wrong direction or place? Is this an area where I need to be more, or more critically, self-aware? If so, what strategies might help me with this?

• Do I ever consciously look to non-obvious or counter-intuitive places when I am trying to deepen understanding or find solutions? If so, does it add anything? If I don't, what is it that stops me?

Prayer

Jesus –
our sometimes
discomforting brother,
too often
we look for you
only in the places
which seem to us

to be sensible
or safe.
May we always be
foolish enough
and brave enough
to also look for you,
and for the signs of your kingdom,
in the counter-intuitive
and at the margins –
those places where
you
have always been at home
and about God's work.
Amen.

Advent 3 – John 1.6–8, 19–28

'What are we looking for?'

Pat Bennett

Introduction

This week we are once again in the company of the Baptist
– although now we are seeing him through the somewhat different lens that John's Gospel provides: where Mark gives us
'the Baptizer', this account presents us with 'the witness'. This
different emphasis means that John supplies some completely
different elements to his namesake's story and these lead to
the third of our Advent 'watching' questions – that of 'What?'
What are we looking for? What expectations do we bring to
our looking and how do these influence what we may or may
not see?

Preparation

Find a copy of the painting *The Sermon of Saint John the
Baptist* by Pieter Bruegel the Elder (Google Arts and Culture
has one where you can zoom in on the details). Examine what
and who people are looking at and jot down any observations.
Do these tie in with what you know about the story of the
Baptist? Why or why not?

Alternatively, get someone to play the 'Who am I?' game
with you (you'll find instructions online if you're not familiar
with it), trying different strategies for what questions you ask
and in what order. What sort of questions or sequences get
you to the answer most quickly? Why do you think these are
successful?

Comment

Note: in what follows, 'John' will always refer to the gospel writer and 'the Baptist' to the figure at the centre of his narrative here.

Today's story of the Baptist and those who go to see him invites us to add 'What?' to the list of questions about looking: What are we looking for – and to what extent does this facet of a complex process affect what we actually can or do see?

The first section of the reading comes from John's prologue – that sweeping poetic introduction to the purpose of his gospel; the second is from the opening narrative through which he begins to advance this aim. Both set out the Baptist's identity and role – the first establishing him in cosmic terms as the divinely commissioned herald of and witness to 'the Light'; the second by underlining who and what he is *not*. Through the repeated depreciations which punctuate the passage (vv. 8, 20, 21, 27 – and later also vv. 30, 31, 33 and 5.30), it is made absolutely clear that, whatever the Baptist's pre-eminence in human terms, he is absolutely and always subordinate to Jesus in terms of the larger narrative: although important and worthy of attention, the Baptist is not the one to whom people should ultimately be looking. This is not to say that those who flocked to see him were wrong to do so, rather that he is only a signpost to direct their looking 'further on and further up'. But to what extent is this what actually happens?

Today's passage focuses on the response of the priests and Levites who come 'from Jerusalem' to look over this strange preacher. We can only surmise as to what drove these emissaries of orthodoxy out into the desert to probe his identity and attempt to categorize him – though it seems to have been connected to ideas about the Messiah. We are told neither what they were expecting to find nor what they actually made of the Baptist and his enigmatic answers. While we can infer from other passages that prominent figures among the Sanhedrin did (both covertly and openly) become disciples of Jesus, the general tenor of John's Gospel suggests that for the most part this was certainly not the case (though we must also bear in mind some of his other agendas too). Indeed, rejection, opposition and plots against Jesus' life were far more typical responses from the religious elite and power brokers. They were, it seems, unable to see, understand or accept that to which the Baptist was pointing.

There can be many reasons why we sometimes don't look further when we need to, or why we can't make sense of what we do see. However, one possibility that the gospel writers consistently highlight is the way our expectations or favoured narratives shape the lenses through which we look: sometimes what we expect or want to see dictates what we can or cannot see. Moreover, we are often largely blind to these influences, taking as 'givens' of the world things which are in reality only our particular interpretations of it. This factor is something that is central to the way Mark unfolds his revelation of Jesus. It's even possible that the Baptist himself may, in some respects at least, have fallen into this error in his expectations of, and preaching about, 'the one who [was] coming after [him]'. Contrast, for example, the different ways in which he and Jesus describe the coming reign of God, and the answers Jesus sends back to the Baptizer's questions from prison in Matthew 11.

Once again then, our gospel passage gives us another lens through which to scrutinize our practice of looking – both as this pertains to situations of conflict and more generally: to what extent is our looking and understanding helped or hindered by the hopes, expectations or world views which (knowingly or unknowingly) we bring to it? Some possible questions for exploring this are suggested below.

Response

• When I am attending to people or things (e.g. a news report or article) in the pursuit of answers or better understandings, do I ever consider who or what it is that I am actually looking for? Does it matter? If so, what things might help me to

be more consciously attentive to this aspect of my practice
of looking?

- To what extent am I aware of the understandings, narratives or agendas which influence what I choose to look at, or
how I read what I see? Have I ever missed or misunderstood
something because of these? Is this an area where I need to
be more, or more critically, self-aware? If so, what strategies
might help me with this?

- Do I ever consciously look to people or things which
wouldn't be my normal 'go to' resources when I am trying
to deepen understanding or find solutions? If so, what, if
anything, has it added? If I don't, what is it that stops me?

Prayer

Jesus –
Sometimes those you encountered
failed to see you properly
because their focus was elsewhere,
or because you were not what they were expecting
or hoping for.

Sometimes we too
fail to see things properly –
because we have not thought
about what we are looking for,
or because what is in our head
blinds us
to what is in front of our eyes.

Help us to look more carefully
so that, when it is needed,
we can see beyond the obvious end point
or the easy answer;
help us to look more keenly
so that, when it matters,
we can see beyond that which is simply

a reflection of our own understanding
or a projection of our own desires or prejudices.

And in looking more faithfully,
may we see the world more truly
and you more clearly
Amen.

Advent 4 – Luke 1.26–38
'Why do we need to look?'

Pat Bennett

At first sight, it might seem that today's passage does not really have anything much to do with looking – after all, Gabriel knows where he is going and what the answer will be, doesn't he? However, the passage (and so one might also say, the Incarnation itself) hinges on an act of profound looking by Mary. Both this, and the fact that we often fail to notice it, point us towards what we could think of as the *meta* question which underlies all our others about looking – that of 'Why do we need to look?' – and also suggest two possible answers for us to consider.

Preparation

Try and break the story down into tiny chapters by identifying different stages in the narrative. What title would you give to each chapter? Alternatively, find different images of the Annunciation and examine the looks and gestures of Gabriel and Mary. Are there differences between the pictures and if so, can you relate them to different moments in Luke's account? Does anything in these exercises make you look at today's gospel passage in a different way?

Comment

Today's familiar text is foundational to the Christian narratives of incarnation and salvation and we can have a tendency to completely collapse the passage into its end point: our attention is so firmly on the 'yes' and its consequences that we make

Mary's acquiescence contiguous with Gabriel's greeting. But actually, there is a complex journey between the two, at the heart of which is an act of the kind of 'collected looking' which we thought about in Advent 1.

One way we can break this down is as a set of three speeches by Gabriel and three corresponding responses in Mary:

G: Greetings   M: questions provoking internal debate
G: Announcement   M: questions provoking external
                         interrogation
G: Explanation   M: consideration followed by consent

We also often read this passage as though Mary's response is a foregone conclusion – an acquiescence to an already inevitable (because divinely ordained) course of events. However, what Luke shows us is someone with *agency* who can consider and weigh up what is being proposed and give or withhold consent; someone who engages in an act of profound, interrogative looking.

The first stage of this comes in response not to the angel's presence but to his address (v. 29). 'Perplexed' somewhat dilutes the force of the Greek *diatarassō* (unique to this passage) which indicates being thoroughly and deeply perturbed. We don't know precisely what images and questions Gabriel's greeting sparks off but Luke's use of the verb *dialogizomai* (here translated as 'pondered') indicates that Mary takes time to deliberate thoroughly with herself,[1] examining all the different things that could lie behind this peculiar encounter and where it might possibly lead. As we will see in the Christmas readings, this type of questioning seems to be a characteristic trait of Luke's Mary.

We have no idea how much time elapses before Gabriel continues (and our tendency to collapse the passage does not help us to hear any pauses in it), but there clearly comes a moment when he sees that Mary is ready to hear more and begins to elaborate his announcement. Now Mary moves to external interrogation – something which St Bonaventure, in his commentary on Luke, approvingly designates 'most prudent'. Unlike Zechariah's 'How will I *know?*' her question is the much more practical 'How will it *happen?*' This response, with its implied willingness to consider further, suggests that a new and differently focused phase of looking has commenced.

Gabriel's answer raises some serious issues for Mary to look at – especially considering her status as a betrothed woman. No wonder she needs to take the time to look, reflect and weigh up, so that she can come to a properly considered decision. In this instance, her looking leads her to answer in the affirmative – she transcends the fear of the likely risks and offers herself freely as a partner in God's proposed plan. But even if it had led her to another answer, it would still have been the same profound and informed act of self- determination.

I want to suggest therefore that the first important answer to the question of 'Why do we need to look?' is 'Because we are *agents*' with control (even if sometimes limited) of our own actions and choices. Therefore, we always have *a responsibility to look* – to consider, to weigh up, to balance, to try to understand – so that, whether in the context of conflict or more generally, we can act in a properly informed way.

The way we typically tend to read this passage points towards a second key answer to the question: we need to *actively look* because we are often very bad at *actually seeing*! This is closely related to what we were thinking about last week: what we see is so often *not* – as we tend to assume – how the world actually is, but much more often a function of the unconsidered assumptions, beliefs and meta narratives which we carry with us. These 'end point' understandings can have so powerful a hold that we collapse the whole narrative into them and fail to look properly at what else might be going on which might expand, enrich or change our way of reading a situation – something which is particularly pertinent in the context of a conflict situation.

So then, we have a responsibility to look properly when we are exploring possibilities or making decisions; and we also need to be willing to look further when we are confronted with situations or people that challenge our understandings, upset our cherished ideas or disrupt our comfortable and comforting narratives. In the response section below there are some suggested questions to consider around this.

Response

- Can I identify with the path that Mary takes from my own experiences? What helps me to see when I need to stop and consider before moving on to the next step? What sorts of questions or perspectives are useful to consider if I am trying to move forwards in understanding a situation and deciding on appropriate action? Is this something I need to get more confident with? If so, is there anything or anyone I can engage with to help me grow in this area?

- Are there particular situations where I feel (or have felt) that I have no choice but to think or act in a certain way, or that I have no responsibility for how I understand or what I do? What effects does this have on these situations? Is this something which needs changing – and if so, how can I make a start with this and who might help me?

- Are there areas where my sense of what is happening, or what a situation entails, is so strong that I feel no need to examine it further or more deeply? What effects does (or might) this have on the evolution of the situation? Do I have ideological touchstones or narrative lodestars which I won't allow to be challenged? If so, why? Are there potential or actual dangers here that I can identify? Are any of these fixed points something which I need to address and, if so, how can I approach this and who might help me if needed?

Prayer

Mary,
interrogator of archangels,
when we would prefer to think
that we simply have no choice,
rather than to acknowledge
our agency
and the responsibilities it brings,
help us to remember
the way you took the time to look
with deep attention
at the situation in which you found yourself;
help us to remember
the way in which you
listened and questioned
with fearless integrity
in order to see
what was being asked of you;
and as we remember your example
may we too
honour the situations
and the questions
which confront us
by looking properly
seeing clearly
and choosing consciously.
Amen.

Further Reading

Denise Levertov's poem 'Annunciation' is a beautiful reflection
on this passage.

Note

1 Definitions and parsings from W. E. Vine, *Expository Dictionary
of New Testament Words* (London: Oliphant, 1978), vol. IV, p. 157,
and vol. III, p. 252.

Nativity of the Lord Propers 1 and 2 – Luke 2.1–20

'What do we do with our seeing?'

Pat Bennett

Introduction

Throughout Advent's season of watching, we have been considering the act of looking and thinking about our own practice in this regard. The Lucan birth narrative allows us to reprise our questions of 'How?' 'Where?' 'What?' and 'Why?' but also to draw them all together into one final question: 'What do we do with our seeing?'

Preparation

Choose a character from the passage (or one whose presence we might infer) and think about what they might see as the events unfold. Then portray this using whatever medium you like: you could compose a short poem, prayer or key word acrostic; or perhaps add a verse to a favourite carol written from their perspective. Or you could make a visual representation in any medium or style that appeals or find some music which expresses the scenes imagined.

Does doing this kind of imagining change the way you read the story, and if so – how?

Comment

One of the questions we have considered in Advent is that of the direction of our gaze and of the need to sometimes look to the margins or to counter-intuitive places. In Advent 2,

Mark placed his herald not at the seat of power but out in the wilderness and there's a similar dynamic here in Luke: 'the whole [Roman] world' of verse 1 delineates a theatre of action which, in terms of both geographical size and people involved, is vast. In contrast, both Galilee and Bethlehem were little more than villages. But it is here, on these insignificant stages far from the centre of Roman power, that the human and cosmically significant action is happening. A similar parallel occurs in verses 8–14 when the angels – beings from high in the heavenly hierarchy – appear, not to the elite and powerful in nearby Jerusalem, but to shepherds on the hillside. Moreover, these lowly hearers become important witnesses to and spreaders of the news of the birth: once again, critical action occurs at the level of the seemingly small and insignificant.

Our questions of 'Where?' and 'How?' also come back into view here: as with the Baptist, the angels are not primarily there to draw attention to themselves but to point the gaze of the lookers elsewhere. In this respect the shepherds do better than some of those who went looking for John (and indeed the disciples in our Advent 1 reading!). They do not get distracted either by the spectacle or by their own emotional reaction to this visitation. Instead, they take on board the content of the message and set off to discover more. Similarly, they take in what they see in the stable and join the dots in such a way that it draws 'all who heard it' into the experience. Moreover, their reportage becomes something which focuses Mary's gaze in a deeper way, helping it to then become part of something which brings us back to our final question: 'What do we do with our seeing?'

Luke uses three different responsive verbs which point us towards some answers. But even before we get to these, the shepherds provide a first and vitally important answer: they take what they see and *act on it*. This, like a stone dropped in a pond, sends out ripples which draw in the looking of others. Luke uses the verb *thaumazō* (to wonder or marvel) to describe this first response to their story. We can imagine a joyful noisiness around its relation and reception, with new listeners being attracted by the buzz as the shepherds return to their flocks. So a second answer to our question is to remind ourselves that there is often an affective element to seeing which we need to recognize and acknowledge and which it is sometimes proper, useful or helpful to act on. We need to be careful here, since this is not about simply allowing our emotions to drive our subsequent actions – but this is where those practices of deep and collected looking which we considered in Advent 1 are important. Awareness of our emotional responses, properly considered, can become part of the cycle of deeper, more developed looking. They can tell us important things about ourselves and our understandings – and the possible need to attend to these – as well as sometimes showing us the necessity for action in response to our seeing.

The two other verbs occur in connection with Mary. The pondering (*dialogizomai*) reflective practice which we noted in Advent 4 is expanded here by Luke's use of *syntēreō* and *symballō* and all three help us to think about a third answer to the question of what we should do with our seeing. *Syntēreō* – translated variously as 'kept' or 'treasured' – means to attend to carefully, to watch over. The Greek word has two constituent components which each contribute something distinctive to its implications: *tēreō* – meaning to attend to carefully, to take care of – carries a strong sense of watching over and preserving.[1] The addition of *syn* denotes things which are brought together by association or process. Its use here gives an additional depth and dimension (which is somewhat lost in the English translation), bringing something of a gestalt feel to what Mary does with 'all these words'.

Although *symballō* is also translated here as 'pondered', it has a different feel to *dialogizomai*. *Ballō* means to scatter, throw or cast into and is the same word that is used in connection with fishing nets in Matthew 4.18 and 13.47. In conjunction once again with *syn* (here transliterated *sym*), it indicates '[putting] one thing with another in considering circumstances'.[2] We can perhaps imagine Mary throwing a mental net to catch all the different thoughts and sensations of her journey to this point

– from annunciation and pregnancy, through the responses of Elizabeth and Joseph to the birth and the visit of the shepherds – and pulling them all together into one place so that she can look at them and see the connections between them and the patterns they form.

Mary thus models an important answer to our final question: what we need to do with our seeing is take it onward (either by ourselves or in conversation with trusted others) into another cycle of looking – revolving things in our mind, weighing up possible explanations, looking at situations in an overarching way or standing back from them in order to see things as a whole, or to help us spot patterns and connections which we might have missed. All of these things will help us to deepen and enrich our understandings – of others, of ourselves, of conflicts, of things currently happening in the world. As we move from a challenging year into one that is likely to be equally testing (though perhaps for different reasons), we have a responsibility, both individually and corporately, to work at building the kind of thick, rich, textured understandings that are both the substance of the kingdom of God and also provide the complex knowledge we need to navigate the times we inhabit. Attention to, and ongoing development of, our practice of looking is a vital part of this.

Response

Revisit some of the questions about looking and seeing which you have asked yourself over the course of these reflections and try and bring them into a further cycle of reflective looking in one of the ways suggested by Mary's approach. Then consider one or more of the following questions (or any others which may occur to you as a result of this further looking).

• Are there connections or patterns which you can see emerging with respect to your own practice of looking? What elements of this do you need to celebrate? Are there facets where you need to do further work?

- If you are reflecting in connection with a particular situation, do you feel that your understanding is becoming more nuanced or more textured as you reflect on your own practice of looking at it?
- Are there any insights from these questions about looking that you can take forward into next year, or into a specific conflict or other situation as a way of developing and deepening the manner in which you engage with it?

Prayer

God be with us in our watching
– and may our looking be attentive and focused.
God be with us in our looking
– and may our seeing be sharp and clear.
God be with us in our seeing
– and may our understanding be deep and rich.
God be with us in our understanding
– and may our doing be courageous and loving.
God be with us in our doing
– and may our living be generous and true.
God be with us in the year to come
– and well,
   and seven times well,
      may we spend ourselves in it. Amen.

Notes

1 W. E. Vine, *Expository Dictionary of New Testament Words* (London: Oliphants, 1978), vol. II, p. 287.

2 Vine, *Expository Dictionary*, vol. III, p. 192.

Advent Year C

Advent Sunday – Luke 21.25–36

Pádraig Ó Tuama

Introduction

There was a time when Advent was just like Lent. The Irish poet Patrick Kavanagh recalls, in his famous poem 'Advent', a childhood memory of when his family would fast in the four weeks leading up to Christmas.[1] Already poor, his farming community would enter into the dark days of December stripped of the few luxuries they had – butter for bread, sugar for tea – all in the aim of opening the heart to the luxuries held within since, 'Through a chink too wide there comes in no wonder.'

As we enter into Advent, we will reflect on how simplicity may be a way of preparing the heart for the radical oncoming of story that is Christmas, by paying attention to the demands of justice, focus and resolution in the readings of Advent.

Comment

It is always striking that the texts for Advent are as stark as they are. The lectionary brings us to some of the more troubled sections of Luke's Gospel for this first week of the season: words about signs in the sun, moon and stars; words about foreboding and shaking and confusion; words about power and glory. The texts propose visions of dystopia.

Before reflecting on the theological insight of the dramatic language, it's worthwhile imagining oneself into the mind of the writer of Luke's Gospel. At this stage, it was supposed that Jesus of Nazareth might come back at any point. As the early gospel tradition developed, some people began to imagine apocalyptic endings any day now and so you find New

Testament texts that are disparaging about, say, marriage, because it's seen as a distraction from the cataclysmic events believed to be just around the corner.

One can read that as a limited understanding of time and religion, but one can also read this as there always being people alive for whom certain events signal to them the end of the world. It may be that the last number of years for many individuals have signalled for them serious political times, with increasing division and rhetoric and public acceptance of boorish performances of masculinities. However, there are entire populations of people who have been living with the consequences of political misrepresentation, manipulation and despotism. The world is always ending – for some populations. And often, those populations are conscious that their drama is ignorable by many.

And so the ancient writer is bringing us into something that is always happening all around us. Awfulnesses are always happening and the opening text of Advent calls the attention of the entire Church to turn towards those places where signs are ominous, worlds are ending, storms and fainting and terriblenesses are all around.

What is extraordinary in this is that the religious imagination is called to a deep integrity: 'Be on guard so that your hearts are not weighed down with dissipation' (v. 34). The faithful are called to not be distracted by fripperies, but also not to be distracted by devastation. To hold deeply to the principle and foundations that will guide you and hold you steady. The four-week drama of Advent builds this sense of foreboding about heavy times and culminates it all in the risk of God becoming incarnate in the body of a small child.

Response

Ignatius of Loyola advised his followers to find, in their prayer, something that would hold them steady. Seek and test different ways, he said, try out a few, so that you can find what will support you to be steady in this life:

That level of prayer is best for each particular individual where God our Lord communicates Himself more. He sees, he knows, what is best for each one and, as he knows all, he shows each the road to take. What we can do to find that way with his divine grace is to seek and test the way forward in many different fashions, so that an individual goes ahead in that way which for him or her is the clearest and happiest and most blessed in this life.

(Ignatius of Loyola)

What supports you in keeping steady: whether in a time of consolation or a time of desolation? Are there ways you could deepen and strengthen this practice during Advent?

Prayer

Jesus, you are always at the world's end,
standing there, with people for whom everything has
    fallen away.
In the hidden corners of humanity, we find you,
abandoned with the abandoned.
May we never forget that the luxuries enjoyed by some
are not enjoyed by all,
and may we be stirred to turn our attention
towards the work of beatitude
for all.
Because this moved you
and moved you
and kept moving you
towards the work of beatitude.
Amen.

Note

1 You can read Kavanagh's poem, and the reflection on it written by poet Carol Rumens for *The Guardian* (16 December 2013), via *The Guardian* website (www.theguardian.com).

Advent 2 – Luke 3.1–6
Pádraig Ó Tuama

Introduction

Luke's Gospel is an extraordinarily political one. Over and over, the writer mentions the names of people in power, referencing their eras, areas of governance and even some of their policies. For week 2 of Advent, we are going to take a quick hop, skip and jump through the political landscape of Luke's Gospel.

Comment

The reading for Advent 1 was filled with warnings about the signs of the times. Now, Luke's text drops us into actual events, describing in detail the political landscape of the times. Even a casual acquaintance with the gospel texts brings some familiarity with the complicated dynamics of conflict in the politics of the day – names such as Herod, Pilate, Judea, Pharisees, Scribes, Samaria, Syrophonecia, Gentile, Rome, all trip off the tongue, even though our knowledge about these geographies, groups and geopolitical realities might be patchy.

For the purposes of clarity about how comfortable Luke's Gospel is in detailing political conflict, here follows some broad brushstroke political history. For detailed reading, you will find some suggested books and links in the further reading section.

About 60 years before the birth of Christ, Rome conquered Jerusalem and 'Herod the Great' – from Samaria – was installed as a client king. The fact that this role was a Samaritan one meant that the role holder was more familiar with Judean practices and religion than the Romans were, yet still distant enough for Roman manipulation. This particular Herod (there were various others) expanded the temple in Jerusalem through heavy taxation and was complicit in the ongoing subjugation of the Jews in Jerusalem and Galilee.

The emperor at the time was Caesar Augustus who lived from 63 BCE to 15 CE and reigned from 44 BCE. Called the 'Son of God' and 'Saviour of the world', songs were sung about how he would 'bring peace'. These names are already alerting us to the political potency at the heart of Mary's Magnificat. Zechariah's song likewise uses images from Exodus while prophesying salvation from enemies (1.71, 73) and those salty prophets, Simeon and Anna, also have the cessation of foreign occupancy and subjection in their hopes. The political context of Luke's Gospel is continued through the narrative of the centurion (7.1–10) and even Jesus predicts the destruction of Jerusalem by opposing armies (21.20–24).

Luke's reference to Quirinius (although problematic in terms of claiming any synchronicity between Mary and Elizabeth's pregnancies) is a clear obvious reference to that census being an occasion for a rebellion led by Judas of Galilee from which came the Zealot movement. That Acts 5.37 mentions Judas the Galilean's revolt in connection with the census indicates the associations that were in the evangelist's mind. All of these political references locate the emerging story of God's saving love amid the reality of political chaos.

On the death of Herod the Great in 4 CE, the Emperor Augustus honoured the terms of his will, placing his son Herod Archelaus over Judea, Samaria and Idumea. This region was referred to – by the Romans – as 'The Tetrarchy of Judea'. However, at the request of the Jewish and Samaritan delegations, the Romans subsequently deposed Archelaus, made border changes and created the 'Judea province'. This enlarged province was ruled by prefects (one of whom was Pilate) until the year 41 CE. From 6–66 there were governors of the Judean province. Pilate was Prefect of Judea, 26–36.

Herod also had three other sons, some of whom are mentioned in this Sunday's gospel reading. Herod Antipas was tetrarch of Peraea and Galilee to 39 CE and his brother Philip ruled areas to the north and the east of the Jordan river. All of this indicates a step-down in power and authority from that which Herod the Great had held. Tetrarch basically means 'a petty prince' – a title that was little more than a plaything for reputation, albeit one that made the lives of some people miserable.

Luke's mention of Lysanias has puzzled biblical historians. Some argue that Luke is making reference to the Lysanias mentioned by Josephus and others that Luke is saying who he thinks should have been ruler at the time, rather than who actually was installed at the time.

The high priests he mentions were another 'in-between' role. They came from among the Jewish people but were appointed by Roman authorities. Annas served as high priest from the year 6 CE to 15. He was young – only 36 by the end of his time as high priest. Yet he remained an important political character, aided by his five sons and his son-in-law Caiaphas (also mentioned in this gospel text). Both Annas and Caiaphas are political actors in the writings of Matthew and John as well as Luke (see Matt. 26.3, 57; John 11.49; 18.13, 24, 28; Acts 4.6)

When Caesar Augustus died in 15 CE, he was succeeded by Tiberias Caesar, under whose reign Jesus was abducted and executed. The Herod of that era is portrayed somewhat passively (23.6–12) because by this stage, Judea is under Pilate, whose bloodthirsty character has been established (13.1). Jesus, a Galilean, who is making his way through the towns and villages (13.22) to Jerusalem, must know that Jerusalem is not a safe place for Galileans.

Even this brief sketch of the political landscape of Luke's Gospel demonstrates the fact that the evangelist locates Jesus firmly within the context of contested territory, temporal powers, political machinations, despotic leadership and disputes about rightful kings. That the gospel progresses in a political vein, moving towards the execution of Jesus as a pretender to the throne (23.2–5, 38), confirms to us that political reality is at the heart of the Gospel of Luke, not a mere backdrop. The words of Zechariah's song – that Jesus is set for the 'rise and the fall of many in Israel' – and Mary's song – casting the mighty from thrones – each lay the foundation for a profoundly politically engaged gospel manuscript, a manuscript that sees the fall of an empire and the glorious inclusion of all in a universal song of salvation that will go from Jerusalem to the ends of the earth.

Response

Today, in our own daily conversations, we make casual references to political realities: 'in the campaign cycle of the general election ...' or 'in the first year of the leadership of ...' or 'during the controversy about ...' or 'the first century after partition ...', using leaders' names as a shorthand for an era of a particular political policy, or evil, or achievement, ambition or deception. To read the text of Luke's Gospel is to be drawn to read the text of our own days – where political realities influence the everyday.

The gospel text calls all of us to be incarnate in our social, cultural, linguistic and political realities and to search for the pathway of justice in these realities. In light of the description of Luke's political landscape, it may be of interest to groups to consider how they would describe their own political landscape of today.

Prayer

God of time,
Time came from the words shaped by your mouth
and then you came into time
in the body of a child:
with a mouth, ears, eyes, legs, arms,
a heart beating,
a stomach aching for food,
and a brain aching for integrity.
In our own time,

give us the wisdom to discern
the signs of the times,
so that we can respond
to the things that will make
life flourish
more and more.
Because you are the one
from whom all life comes
and with whom all life flourishes
more and more.
Amen.

Further reading

All of the information above has been gleaned from the following scholars, to whose study and intelligence much is due. Any
mistakes are entirely mine.

Sean Freyne, *Galilee, Jesus and the Gospels*, Dublin: Gill and
    Macmillan, 1988.
Joel B. Green, *The Gospel of Luke*, Grand Rapids, MI: Eerd-
    mans, 1997.
Joel B. Green, Scott McKnight, I. Howard Marshall (eds),
    Dictionary of Jesus and the Gospels, Leicester and Downers
    Grove, IL: InterVarsity Press, 1992.
Richard A. Horsley, *The Liberation of Christmas: The Infancy
    Narratives in Social Context*, New York: Crossroad, 1989.
Elisabeth Schüssler Fiorenza, *Jesus: Miriam's Child, Sophia's
    Prophet: Critical Issues in Feminist Christology*, New York:
    Continuum, 1994.
James M. Scott, *Geography in Early Judaism and Christianity*,
    Cambridge: Cambridge University Press, 2002.
Steven M. Sheeley, *Narrative Asides in Luke–Acts*, Sheffield:
    Sheffield Academic Press, 1992.
Robert C. Tannehill, *The Shape of Luke's Story*, Eugene, OR:
    Cascade Books, 2005.

Advent 3 – Luke 3.7–18

Pádraig Ó Tuama

Introduction

For the third week of Advent, we find our liturgical imaginations turned towards serious things: money and the company we keep. These are the topics for this Sunday's drama. And the stage? The wilderness, the region around the Jordan. The characters on this stage are John the Baptist, surrounded by crowds, with two examples – tax collectors and soldiers – indicating the breadth of that curious population.

Luke's Gospel is known as a gospel of universal appeal. Working within the particularity of the revelation of God to the Jewish people, the message of Luke's Jesus builds in its appeal and relevance to populations beyond just Jesus' co-religionists. And here, early in the gospel's unfolding story, we already see seeds of this broad appeal.

This Sunday is known as Gaudete Sunday – Gaudete meaning 'rejoice' or 'joyful'. For those who fast through Advent, it's a break from the fast, a foretaste of what's to come. The texts point to the true centre of rejoicing: a community of diversity held together in integrity, and care for those at the margins.

Comment

The gospel tradition regularly practises what has come to be known as 'defamiliarization' – from the Russian word *ostranenie* (остранение). Popularized by the Russian formalist Victor Shklovsky in 1917, defamiliarization suspends, twists and turns on its head the familiar or everyday way of looking at the world by substituting a new, unfamiliar frame of reference. It causes us to stumble and in so doing it leads us to begin to take notice. Literary theologian James Resseguie notes how the gospels employ this technique of using the sayings of Jesus and the words of outsiders – widows, Gentiles, Samaritans, tax collectors, etc. – to 'deform' the ideological perspectives of the dominant culture, that is, the religious authorities, the power-ful and the wealthy landowners.[1]

Here, in the wilderness, away from the city, we have a gather-ing of the unusual. We see John – a strange man – surrounded by 'crowds'.[2] And Luke is at pains to characterize the crowds in two ways: through tax collectors and soldiers. One category was considered to have rescinded their rights of belonging, the other belonged to an occupying foreign force. And this is the family of God that is being welcomed in. At this stage in Luke's Gospel, there are no forbidden professions; all that's asked is that the people are fair in their work. Luke is not keen to paint a perfect picture of the world. As was evidenced in the political landscape outlined in the readings of the Second Sunday of Advent, Luke understands the mess of political reality. He doesn't envision utopia, but he does demand – through the voice of John the Baptist – serious relational reciprocality from the ragtag population gathered out on the edge of the city. If your heart is as cold as a stone, that's OK in the economy of this gospel, because God can even make children out of stones, and give them living hearts.

For Luke, primary integrity is shown in your relationship with money. Note the financial focus in the instructions to both tax collectors and soldiers:

> Even tax collectors came to be baptized, and they asked him, 'Teacher, what should we do?' He said to them, 'Collect no more than the amount prescribed for you.' Soldiers also asked him, 'And we, what should we do?' He said to them, 'Do not extort money from anyone by threats or false accusation, and be satisfied with your wages.'

Luke's Gospel was written 40 years after the events it is describ-ing. For the writer, the events being foretold in the mouth of John the Baptist have already occurred: Jerusalem is sacked.

And what will be left in this? People who support others, people who are not rich, but who are good to each other while recovering from the ravages of war.

This is less about conflict resolution and more about the kinds of behaviours that will keep people alive in the aftermath of conflict, or the kinds of practices to help us survive conflict. As a Gaudete, it is not cheery, but it is true and is the kind of civic reciprocality that will keep us alive long enough to form the joy of human community together.

Response

In the gathering of humanity sketched by Luke we hear that he highlights 'even' tax collectors and sinners. Many, if not most, of us have groupings of people we might consider to be separated from us: whether because of politics or because of associations.

Who are the people you would go to pains to avoid? What does this reveal about you?

What is the pilgrimage to the places of wilderness, survival, generosity and community that this gospel text might call you to?

Prayer

Jesus, cousin of John,
like your cousin, you envisioned communities
made up with all kinds of people.
And with that imagination, you gathered
all kinds of people around you ...
even us.
Call us towards the kinds of communities
that will shape and change us
towards a greater diversity, a greater justice,
a wiser distribution of power.
Because this is the Jordan
where we'll find you

and people like you.
Amen.

Notes

1 James Resseguie, *Narrative Criticism of the New Testament: An Introduction* (Grand Rapids, MI: Baker Academic, 2005), p. 34ff.

2 The four evangelists use the term 'crowd' to different purposes; sometimes depicting the crowd as skeptical and threatening, other times using the same term to refer to curiosity, mildness and collective fear. Luke's references to 'crowd' are worthy of a study in itself: Luke 3.7, 10; 4.42; 5.1, 3, 15, 19, 29; 6.17, 19; 7.9, 11, 12, 24; 8.4, 19, 40, 42, 45; 9.11, 12, 16, 18, 37; 11.14, 27, 29; 12.1, 13, 54; 13.14, 17; 14.25; 18.36; 19.3, 39; 22.6; 22.47; 23.4, 48.

Advent 4 – Luke 1.39–55

Pádraig Ó Tuama

Introduction

The final Sunday of Advent is upon us. Appropriately, the text combines extraordinary joy with deep justice. Mary – a young woman who has just crossed occupied territory 'with haste' – has arrived at her cousin Elizabeth's. In a chapter filled with masculinist military references, Luke chooses to amplify the story of two women, going so far as to silence the voice of Zechariah, the priest.

Mary and Elizabeth – prophets, evangelists, witness-bearers and theologians both – have an elemental recognition of each other's story, and Luke puts this extraordinary Magnificat in the mouth of Mary, placing her alongside all the other prophets who have seen the dynamism of God in the midst of the ordinary things of life.

Comment

The throw-away references to Mary crossing the hill country of Judea 'with haste' has often been explained as an indication of Mary's excitement to visit her cousin. However, as we have seen, Luke's Gospel unfolds on an extraordinarily political and militaristic landscape. There are soldiers and tetrarchs and territories everywhere – no wonder Luke has Mary crossing the country at speed.

I cannot think of Mary without thinking of a story of pilgrimage and peace amid tensions and complications. A few years ago, I spent a day with a group of Jews and Muslims in London. They meet monthly, taking time to speak, to hear, to listen, to understand, to get to know each other, to tell difficult stories, to ask difficult questions, to work hard to disagree well.

They have an interest in reconciliation and being witnesses to religious diversity across traditions sometimes fractured in relationships.

We gathered in a room at the top of a building. At the beginning of the day, we shared introductions, followed by reflecting on the story of the group – hearing why the group had met, what keeps them meeting and what keeps them coming back.

This group of people represent the tensions and pains of our world. They had taken painful pilgrimages – often against their will – to bear witness to their hope. Somebody comes from a region torn apart by violent conflict; somebody lives with an injury after a bomb; somebody's family rejects their interfaith engagements. Somebody said they are lonely, somebody invited them to an evening out. Somebody says, 'I have more problems with the tensions within my own religion than I do with the tensions between people of different religions.' Everybody laughed. Bread was broken. Pain was shared. Glad and generous hearts.

We met for a full day. As we came close to lunch, someone went to a kitchen to make rice to accompany the curry. While they were doing that, some of the Muslims prepared a space in the room to pray. They invited anyone who wished to join them, and so, while Muslim friends praised the greatness of God – prayer mats facing in the same direction – others sat quietly in meditation, or prayer, or reflection. Someone was preparing a table for food while the only noises were ancient prayers, the rustle of clothes as people bowed, the sound of breathing.

Over lunch, we spoke of Mary, as it was a feast day of Mary in the Christian calendar. Someone asked me what the text was and we discussed that. Somebody else said, 'Do you know that Mary has a full Surah about her in the Qu'ran? ... Would you like to hear it?' Everyone was quiet. She said, 'I can remember it.' Everybody stopped eating. She recited the Surah, from memory, by heart.

Mary is a being described as the figure upon whom a religious tradition turns. The theologian Yves Congar refers to

Mary as both 'the final figure of Old Testament History' and 'the original cell of the new creation in Christ by which all humanity share in the glory of God in a new, graced way'. Luke is choosing to describe the central turning point of salvation history through the story of two women – one young and one old – living under the compromising circumstances of a country caught up in the conflict of empire.

In the Qur'an, no other woman is given as much attention as Mary; indeed the 19th Chapter of the Qur'an is named after her, and of the 114 Surahs, Mary is one of eight people who has a Surah named after her. The sacred text from the Qur'an – as sung by the woman in London – moved the group immensely.

In the Gospel of Luke, Mary is at once a person of extraordinary character and a person caught up in the ordinary things of life under occupation. Karl Rahner says that Mary's life, in the midst of the complications, poverty and sorrow it contained, gives us the courage to recognize that holiness is not so heavenly and ethereal, but is ordinary, and this helps us to see that the ordinary everyday can be the seat of grace in our lives.

Mary's life – like many lives – exists between the dynamics of faith and conflict. Affected by the empire of the time, her vision is beyond time – holding an old story and a new one in her person. Luke peppers the text with references to Mary that indicate the unique place she occupies in time and Christian theology. Mary's journey across the hill country, and her arrival at her cousin's house, are narrated in ways that portray her as the Ark of the Covenant. Compare the following texts:

'And why is this granted to me, *that the mother of my Lord should come to me?*' (Luke 1.43, ESV).
'[David] said, *"How can the ark of the Lord come to me?"*' (2 Sam. 6.9, ESV).

'For behold ... the babe in my womb *leaped*' (Luke 1.44).
'Michal ... looked out of the window and saw King David *leaping*' (2 Sam. 6.16, ESV).

'And Mary remained with her about *three months*' (Luke 1.56, ESV).
'The ark of the Lord remained in the house of Obed-edom the Gittite *three months*' (2 Sam. 6.11, ESV).

She is the person held between received stories and emerging ones. In her – as in that brave community of friends meeting across traditions – stories meet and are held together in an integrity that calls for justice and resolution. In the ordinariness, bravery, suffering and determination of her life, we see God's saving action in a story arcing towards beatitude.

Response

There's an old anecdote that an order of nuns were expelled from a certain country because their daily recitation of the Magnificat was deemed to be a challenge to a dictatorial government. It's probably not entirely true, but I think there's truth in it nonetheless. Many orders of religious women have spoken truth to power and have found their home in the Magnificat, a prayer they pray by heart every day. Recite the Magnificat and consider how it's a psalm of challenge, of resistance and of hope for a changed order.

Prayer

God of the ground,
in Mary's words we hear a vision that could change the world
and through Mary's life you changed, too.
Give us the imagination to believe
that even though we are not mighty
you can raise up songs from the dust
that change powers
for good.
Because you did this
through the *yes* of one woman.
Amen.

The Nativity of the Lord – Years A, B and C

The same texts are set for Propers 1, 2 and 3 across all the years of the lectionary cycle. In addition, there is an overlap in the texts from Luke set for Propers 1 and 2. In this section there are two reflections based on the Luke passage and one on the passage from John set for Proper 3. There is also a reflection for Propers 1 and 2 with the themed set for Advent Year B (p. 63).

Nativity of the Lord Proper 1 – Luke 2.1–14

Janet Foggie

Introduction

The good news of Christmas Morning is upon us. Children have hurried out of bed, presents have been opened and joy abounds. Yet for many, Christmas is also a time of changes, of experiencing or remembering loss or bereavement, a time of looking back as well as celebrating. We read the passage today considering the idea of an angel, and the role of the angel in this story which brings the heavenly host to sing to the holy family.

Comment

What is an angel? The Christmas story is imbued with a direct divine intervention in the form of angels sent as messengers. For us, an angel is usually represented by a pre-pubescent girl in a white costume with tinsel in her hair. This Victorian convention of the angelic female child follows a long history of Christmas plays which can be traced back to the first crib scene, the introduction of which is attributed to St Francis of Assisi. The angels in the nativity play are usually drawn from the angel who appears to Mary, and those which sing to the shepherds, both of whom appear in Luke.

The angel has also passed into modern contemporary culture: Abba, Robbie Williams and Ed Sheeran have all written hugely popular modern songs using the idea of an angel to express hope for change, loss and a belief in an afterlife. Abba's 'I have a dream' makes a connection between believing in fairy tales and in angels as a force for good: 'I believe in angels/

Something good in everything I see.' Robbie Williams' song 'Angels' is now over 20 years old – the first draft was written by Ray Heffernan after his partner suffered a miscarriage. In the song, lost love is a love for angels. Loss and the intervention of angels are readily understood by people today and it is a song commonly requested at funerals.

Ed Sheeran wrote 'Supermarket Flowers' about the loss of his grandmother, describing her as an angel, and referring to her journey to heaven as being a moment of rejoicing: Heaven will say, 'Hallelujah' as she is admitted there. Again, this is becoming a very popular song for funerals as people identify with the sentiment of losing a much-loved older female family member.

These popular concepts of angels are carried by many into the understanding of the congregation of the nativity play and its function. Family bonds of love, shared times together and intergenerational experiences all typify our Christmas experience within church, and so it is natural to wish to soften the darker side of the Christmas tale with angels who mediate grief, provide good news and a link between our mortal lives and eternal life.

In the metaphor of the angel in Matthew's story, we have a direct intervention by the divine in the human experience. As we can see from the use of angels in popular music, it is an idea that is widely understood as a helpful bridge between those things of faith which we cannot explain and the reality of lived experiences of loss and major life events.

This Christmas may be a time of remembered loss, a time of changing events or of dreaming a new future. The metaphor of an angel bearing such a message or mediating such a pain carries the reality of the gospel into our unique experience and speaks to us of the love of God for each of us.

Response

For some church members today, there is a perceived conflict between the culture and traditions of church and pop songs, social media and modern culture. It is hard when writing Christmas material to bridge the gap between the popular culture of the parents, who will come to see a child in a nativity play, and some of the older regular members of the church. What popular songs could be played in church to demonstrate aspects of the Christmas story? Are they from the 1980s or the 2010s? Why not try to compose a Christmas service using only cultural references, music and songs post-2010? Speak to the congregation about worship now and the gospel being alive to the culture of today.

How does the metaphor of the angel as God's messenger speak to you? Have you ever seen an angel? Or heard one in a dream? Or are you sceptical of angels as a reality and see them as a poetic or literary device to explain those times our lives take a dramatic turn?

Prayer

God who sent the angel,
send us out from worship
to serve the world around us
to understand it as it is
and to offer to our world
the gift of Christmas
in our love.
Amen.

Nativity of the Lord Proper 2 – Luke 2.1–20

Pádraig Ó Tuama

Introduction

Today, for Christmas, we will introduce some conflict into the way we read Luke's version of the Christmas story: there was plenty of room in the inn! The way we tell a story – or read a story – is powerful and can spell the delight or the doom of those people whose lives are narrated in that story. To narrate a story is a role that must be taken with great integrity.

So today, for Christmas, a blessing of hospitality – one that might introduce conflict to your story.

Comment

For Christmas, we are pleased to introduce some conflict to you – notably a conflict in how we can read the text from Luke's Gospel, that text beloved of Christmas pageants everywhere.

You may have been a shepherd in a pageant. You may have attended one in a school or church recently. Or you may have seen beautiful renditions like the one told by wonderful small humans from St Paul's Church in Auckland, New Zealand.[1] They are charming, beautiful, full of such potential and pleasure in the art of the imagination.

However, there is a necessary conflict we wish to introduce. The way we tell Bible stories is often unfaithful to the text. Luke's Gospel – from which much of the story comes – records no stable, no animals and, most importantly, no inhospitality. Luke, normally so kind and gracious, giving so much time to stories of the marginalized, rushes through the birth of Jesus as if it were of little importance. Joseph and Mary had gone to Bethlehem for the census and:

> While they were there, the time came for her to deliver her child. And she gave birth to her firstborn son and wrapped him in bands of cloth, and laid him in a manger, because there was no place for them in the inn.

See? No animals, no inhospitality, no stable. Sorry/not sorry.

There is a deeper story here, one of kind hospitality. And it hinges upon the word 'inn'. The word used here is a curious one. In biblical Greek there are two words for inn – *kataluma* and *pandocheion*. When we hear the word 'inn' we tend to think of a resting house, with an owner, and rooms, kind of like a medieval hostel where you could rest your horses and get a room for a night.

Luke uses both words for 'inn' throughout his gospel. When he is telling the story of the mobbed man who was so helped by the Samaritan, he uses the word *pandocheion*, which does indeed translate as that kind of 'inn' – a resting house, with an owner, and rooms. However, here in the nativity story, when the family find out that there is no place in the 'inn', the word used is *kataluma* – which was a different thing altogether. Most people of the time lived in a one-room structure. In that room there was space for living, sleeping and a fireplace. Additionally, the animals were brought in for the night to that same space – for their protection and because of the warmth they gave. Those houses lucky enough to have a *kataluma* had an additional upper room. This room, the *kataluma*, the upper room, could be rented out, like the ancient world's equivalent of Airbnb.

Joseph and Mary, arriving in Bethlehem, could not find a *kataluma*. They were in Bethlehem because that's where Joseph's kinsfolk were. So they had the baby and laid him in the manger. The manger would have been where mangers always were: in the living space of a family, a family who made room for Joseph, Mary and Jesus in their own home. Presumably they were relatives of Joseph.

This is much more ordinary, much less dramatic. And, importantly, this reading is much less offensive to the good people of the Holy Land who are aghast at Western tellings of the nativity story that imply that anyone would turn away any woman – whether kinsfolk or not – in the last moments of pregnancy.

Luke's story of *kataluma* continues. At the end of the gospel, *kataluma* arises once again. Jesus and his friends meet for a meal – a last supper – and this time, he makes it to the *kataluma*. The word can also be translated as 'an upper room'.

The way we tell the story tells so much. Stars and angels and joy and delight. Also, inhospitality, cruelty, unintended insult and limitation. We must always be attentive to the edges of our own storytelling. Attractive as it may be to children, and lodged as it may be upon the portrayed scenes of religious Christmas cards, it is simply incorrect to think that Mary and Joseph were forced into a stable. They found shelter in the kindness of people, presumably Joseph's kin in his traditional homeland of Bethlehem. This kindness was so ordinary, so expected, so taken for granted that Luke, the gentle evangelist, did not even make mention of the family whose home was used for what we consider to be the birthing of a god-child to confused parents.

But the telling of the story can make many things possible. To tell the story in one way implies something about the character of people in Bethlehem at the time – that they would send a woman to a stable to give birth. It is necessary to introduce conflict into received readings of this story: by doing that, we might realize that every moment of human encounter, every small demonstration of hospitality carries within it the possibility for incarnation. We can see that human touch, the actual touching of flesh and flesh, is in itself sacred. We can also see that religion at its best can communicate an honour for the ordinary, the everyday, the unremarkable – and find something remarkable in the midst of this parochial normality.

We are capable of so many things, we humans. Hospitality and hostility. Kindness and cruelty. What prophet said that? I don't know. I made it up. If one didn't say it, one should have said it. It may not be true, but it doesn't make it untrue.

Response

As a small act of theological imagination, consider what a nativity play – carried out by cute children wrapped in over-sized draperies – that portrayed actual hospitality might look like. No drama, no foils – just people under occupation doing what people have done for millennia: looking after each other.

Prayer

Jesus of Nazareth
you were born in the home of people
whose names history has forgotten.
Presumably they lent cloths and clothes
to your internally displaced parents.
We bless and honour all
who show hospitality –
they make the message of Christmas
relevant for every day.
People in shelters, refuges,
people in the welcome centres at prisons,
in the waiting rooms of health centres,
people on streets whose door is always open
for the neighbour who needs a tea and hospitality.
We bless and honour them.
We bless and honour them.
Because this is where you were born,
and are born every day.
And you
bless and honour them.
Amen.

Note

1 St Paul's Auckland, 'The Christmas Story', *YouTube*, www.you tube.com/watch?v=kWq6ooyrHVQ (accessed 14 June 2021).

Nativity of the Lord Proper 3 – John 1.1–14

Pat Bennett

Introduction

Unlike Matthew and Luke, John has no infancy narratives, instead presenting the arrival of Jesus in sweeping cosmological terms. The resulting prologue to his gospel is perhaps one of the best-known and best-loved passages of the New Testament. John's beautifully crafted, mysterious, poetic masterpiece provides us with a dense and deep introduction to the multi-faceted Jesus who strides through his gospel. As with the Lucan birth narratives, 'conflict' is not a theme we tend to associate with this particular Christmas reading, despite the hint in verses 10 and 11 of a less than positive reception to the appearance of the Word. Once again, though, there are elements and dynamics within the text that we can use to help us delve into aspects of what developing a spirituality of conflict entails. This reflection will focus on two themes – the first implicit in the opening five verses with their creation-story resonances and the second at the heart of verse 14.

Preparation

Read the passage several times, including once out loud, and simply savour its cadences. Then choose one verse which particularly draws your attention and reflect on the following questions: what does it tell you about Jesus? In light of that, does it help you to understand anything about your own place in the world and about the consequences of that in terms of how you live your life?

Comment

The way in which John uses his prologue to establish Jesus' divine credentials as God's *Logos* is not unlike a typical piece of midrashic commentary: the first verses are an exposition on the opening of the book of Genesis, using the Wisdom passage in Proverbs 8.22–31 as the interpretative key.[1] In directing attention back to 'the beginning', John invites his readers to recall the creation story and the fact that before 'things came into being' under the direction of God and his *Logos*, a state of primordial chaos existed. In fact, the narrative of Genesis 1 is primarily concerned with the imposition of order on chaos: from God's first move against the primal threat of the *Tohuwabohu* (Genesis 1.2), via a series of separations and namings, disorder is progressively driven out and order and structure gradually achieved. As such, the text reflects the priestly perspective that chaos is the great menace to creation.[2] There is a strong link here with the key Old Testament concept of *shālôm*, which was deeply and organically connected to understanding the world as a place from which chaos has been driven back by God. The pursuit and realization of *shālômic* relationships within society was seen as a vital component of keeping those forces, with their destructive potential for individual, society and nation, at bay.

There is much here that we could also apply to dealing with conflict situations – separating out, recognizing and naming aspects of what is happening or bringing light to bear on hidden dimensions, etc., can play a role in attempts to bring order and resolution to a situation of disagreement or strife. However, a third element in John's prologue might suggest that this is not necessarily the first point of application for such tactics.

The final verse of the passage is critical in a number of ways to what John seeks to convey both in this prologue and the gospel that follows it. As already noted, John makes no reference to the birth of Jesus per se, concentrating instead on establishing Jesus' relationship to God. However, in this final verse he asserts the incarnational nature of Jesus' presence on earth – the reality of his enfleshed existence – in a very strong and unambiguous way. In using the same root word – *ginomai* (to come into existence, begin to be, receive being) – as is used in verse 3 in relation to the rest of creation, he underlines the humanity of Jesus: that he comes into existence just as we do and that he occupies and acts in the earthly, human realm, just as we do. In John's Gospel 'the flesh' is not a locus of corruption but a place of potential: Jesus constantly reaches out and restores the flesh of others, releasing new possibilities in the process; he offers his flesh for the life of the world; it is in his own fleshly existence that God is revealed. 'Whoever has seen me has seen the Father,' he says in response to Philip in 14.9. Ultimately it is through his own flesh that he teaches his disciples what it means to be faithful to God and the imperatives of his kingdom, what it means to love those with whom we are connected 'to the end'.

Perhaps, then, any attempt to bring progress or resolution in a particular situation needs to begin in our own flesh with an examination of ourselves and our relationships to people, processes and ideas – since it is as embodied humans, not disembodied theoreticians, that we act as agents in the world. We need to look critically at our own relationships with others and see whether and to what extent these are governed by the principles of *shālôm*; we need to recognize and name dysfunctions and prejudices rooted in our own experience which might influence how we respond or act – and offer these to God for healing and transformation; we need to become more aware of areas in our thinking and understanding which need further illumination from the light of the gospel – and open them up to its radical challenges. Only when we have opened our own chaos to the light of God will we be in a position to contribute to driving back disorder elsewhere.

Response

Think about different groups of people whom you 'live among' – family, friends, work, church, groups to which you belong, etc. Choose a couple and either list the names of the people with whom you are connected in that context or draw a relational web of those links. Then think about the people and connections represented: are there any that have been particularly helpful or life-enhancing? How might you celebrate these? Are there any that need attention or repair? How might you nurture these? Spend some time praying for the people with whom you are connected.

Prayer

Inspiring Word
move over the chaos within me
calling forth form and order
that I may know you in my shaping
and, in the shaping,
surrender my life to yours.

Illuminating Word
pierce the darkness within me
calling forth insight and understanding
that I may know you in my seeing
and, in seeing,
follow the way of your kingdom.

Incarnate Word
indwell the life within me
calling forth passion and purpose
that I may know you in my living
and, in living,
embody you for the world.
Amen.[3]

Notes

1 See Daniel Boyarin's essay, 'John's Prologue as Midrash' in *The Jewish Annotated New Testament* (Oxford: Oxford University Press, 2011), pp. 546–9.

2 Gerhard von Rad, *Old Testament Theology: The Theology of Israel's Historical Traditions* (Louisville, KY: Westminster John Knox Press, 2001), p. 144.

3 Prayer © P. Bennett. Published in *Hay and Stardust*, Wild Goose Publications, www.ionabooks.com, used with permission.

The Holy Name of Jesus – Luke 2.15–21

Ruth Harvey

Introduction

Jesus the infant is formally named at his circumcision. What does this story have to offer us today about rites of passage around naming and its significance in a Christian context? And what power or impact do names, or naming, have in the context of war and conflict?

Preparation

Consider your own name, or names, the reasons they were given to you and what they mean.

Comment

The naming of a child is a testing act by all accounts. Deciding on a name that will be with a child for life is weighty. In the case of Jesus' naming, however, there was no doubt. Earlier in this gospel (Luke 1.31), Gabriel tells Mary: 'Behold, you will conceive in your womb and bear a son, and you shall name him Jesus.' And in Matthew's version of the story (Matthew 1.21, ESV), the angel instructs Joseph: 'you shall call his name Jesus, for he will save his people from their sins,' linking the naming of this child to the salvation of all people. The naming of this child was no random act.

The name Jesus used in the English New Testament comes from the Latin form of the Greek name *Iēsous*, itself a rendition of the Hebrew *Yeshua* (ישוע) related to the name Joshua. The Hebrew root of this name is 'rescue, deliver', which has led to translations including 'salvation' and 'saviour', linking back to the angel's words to Joseph.

The use of the name Emmanuel (God is with us), prophesied in Isaiah (7.14), is not mentioned in the New Testament, but is echoed in Matthew (28.20, KJV) when Jesus says: 'I am with you always, even unto the end of the world.'

The deliberate naming of this child, who became the Christ after his resurrection, explains why there has been such a focus on, and veneration of, the Holy Name of Jesus since the first century. Picked up in prayer rituals ('we pray in and through the name of Jesus Christ'), underpinning the lives of religious communities (e.g. the Society of the Holy Name) and liturgical rituals (e.g. the Feast of the Holy Name), this short passage in Luke's Gospel carries great weight.

Used in petition and prayer, the Holy Name carries weight and gives power: 'If you ask the Father anything in my name he will give it you' (John 16.23); 'Those who "call on the name of the Lord" will be saved' (Romans 10.13). But what of names and naming today? T. S. Eliot, in his 'Naming of Cats', famously devoted a series of poems to the rituals and meanings of naming, underscoring the weight that formal and informal names carry, and testifying to the fact that the meanings of names can influence or describe actions and characteristics of individuals.

In many cultures, our name carries a signifier that can harm or mark us in a destructive way. In situations of conflict, names rooted in our religious or historical tradition can mark us as part of the 'in' or 'out' group according to our stance. Names given with pride, delight and reverence can become names weighted with fear – a terrifying public marker of a stance or belonging that can evoke violence, and even lead to death.

In parts of our world, this 'marking', or public identification, is taken to a different level with the act of scarification, where identity is etched deep into the brow. At a certain age, often as young teenagers, deep scars are etched into the forehead or brow or body to mark tribal, clan or family belonging. A process perhaps initiated to induce pride has, in some cases, fuelled horrific war. This process and other forms of public identification (e.g. the yellow star in World War 2) has meant

that in some cultures, where peaceful life has been disrupted
by ethnic cleansing, tribal warfare or violence, our identity has
been etched into our brows or pinned on our clothing in such a
way that we cannot escape violence or even death.

'Sticks and stones can break my bones, but words will
never hurt me' was a playground chant in my childhood.
Yet in sectarian Scotland, we knew, without blinking, that
children with certain names would go to particular schools
and that the shared playground between our Catholic and non-
denominational primary schools had to be monitored at breaks
to stop tribal fighting across religious lines. Calling names may
not have broken many bones, but the names with which we
had been born could swiftly turn from badges of honour to
placards on our brow inciting fear and violence.

Response

What does your name signify in terms of your tribal, cultural
or religious belonging?

Consider the power of names in religious contexts where
they have been used to incite violence or war. Consider other
public identifiers (e.g. the yellow star, or scarification) where
symbols of pride have been used to aid massacre. What
responses have our churches made in the past to bring peace in
these contexts and to reach for a deeper identity? What further
responses could be made?

Prayer

Holy God, Prince of Peace;
Emmanuel, God with us;
Wonderful Counsellor –

Loving God of many names
we bring our whole selves to you:
the whole of us, known by you before birth,
the whole of us, known before naming.

You know and love us beyond
label, pedigree, lineage or genetics.

In and through your holy name
we pray for all scarred or killed
because of their name,
and ask your blessing on all
new-borns named before you today.
Amen.

Reflections for Ash Wednesday and the Season of Lent

Lent Year A

Ash Wednesday – Matthew 6.1–6, 16–21

Trevor Williams

Introduction

Ash Wednesday – and the start of the 40-day journey of Lent. What memories, stories and experiences do you bring to this day? What is it about for you: sin, failure, despair, death – or something different?

Religion often gets a bad press, and for good reason. So much violence throughout the world has a religious motivation. As someone living in Northern Ireland, I am used to people asking, why are Catholics and Protestants fighting each other?

Is there good religion and bad religion? If so, how do we know what is what? And how do we know if what we are following or practising is bad religion? These are some of the issues that Jesus is addressing in this reading from the Sermon on the Mount.

Comment

If you are not 'pious', don't take comfort in the beginning of our reading. The word translated 'pious' is actually 'righteousness' or 'justice'. Jesus is not talking about the act of religious observance per se, but an underlying attitude to which we all too easily succumb. The attitude to which Jesus is referring has to do with our concern about how we appear to others.

There is a prevalent myth that each of us are individuals, that we make up our own minds and make choices freely and independently. René Girard, the late French literary theorist and anthropologist, has countered this view. He asserts that we always live in relation to others and that our desires are deeply influenced and shaped by them.[1] As an example, we may suddenly desire an object because someone we know has just bought it: we have a sense of being deprived – we need it, so we must have it, or something better! This rivalry is a form of conflict and like all conflict it can easily escalate – sometimes into violence. This reading shows how our religious practice can also be motivated by rivalry and an attendant desire to demonstrate our superiority over others.

In verses 2–4 we have the contrast. Our religious practice may indeed win the admiration of others and that, we are told by Jesus, is our reward. To act freely, lovingly, for the good of the other alone, in secret, will go unnoticed by others – but 'your Father who sees in secret will reward you'. In verses 5–6, the same principle is applied to prayer. We should pray in secret, not for show. In verses 7–8, when we fast, we should freshen up so that our fast can remain free from rivalry with others.

For me, René Girard has given us an insight into a particular aspect of human existence – our rivalry with others. It is this rivalry that leads to the prevalence of violence in our relationships, homes, communities, countries and nations.

There is another way, however – the way of the Gospel, the way of freedom. The free gift of God's love in Jesus Christ secures our identity beyond all doubt. As we find our identity through the free gift of God's love, we are freed from the instinct driving us to rival others and instead are liberated to love them as God has loved us.

So the verses in today's reading from the Sermon on the Mount are not so much commands that must be obeyed, but signposts to freedom in Christ. Where we seek our security and identity will be a choice between investing our lives in what is passing, disposable and corruptible, or finding our identity as a gift from God made real for us in the person of Jesus Christ; that is, to find lasting fulfilment:

Do not store up for yourselves treasures on earth, where moth and rust consume and where thieves break in and steal; but store up for yourselves treasures in heaven, where neither moth nor rust consumes and where thieves do not break in and steal. For where your treasure is, there your heart will be also.

Response

You might like to consider one or more of the following:

- Think about a conflict you have experienced. Did it escalate? If so, did rivalry between the participants play a part? What kind of action would have broken the rivalrous spiral? What has this to do with hypocrisy (verse 16)?
- Among your relationships can you identify any which have a tendency towards rivalry? If so, what can you do to free yourself from that rivalry?
- These verses refer to religious observance and worship. What are your thoughts about rivalry in the Christian community? Is this something you have experienced? Are there steps you can take to counter this?

Prayer

Loving God, who in Jesus Christ
welcomes us as warmly as sons and daughters,
may we so rest in the riches of your unconditional love,
that our instinct to rival others
is transformed by the impulse to love them
as you have loved us.
Amen.

Note

1 If you want to read more of Girard's writing on the subject of rivalry, see René Girard, *Deceit, Desire and the Novel: Self and Other in Literary Structure* (Baltimore, MD: John Hopkins University Press, 1961).

There is also an extensive website (www.girardianlectionary.net) looking at the gospels through Girard's work on mimetic theory.

Lent 1 – Matthew 4.1–11

Pádraig Ó Tuama

Introduction

In 2000, Columba Press published Cecelia Clegg and Joe Liechty's extraordinary volume *Moving Beyond Sectarianism*.[1] This study – the result of years of research, group engagement, dialogue and analysis – explored the phenomenon of British–Irish sectarianism and proposed ways to a) understand the impulses towards it and b) move beyond those impulses. The authors proposed that there is a 'scale' of sectarianism. This scale has eleven parts – moving from 'You are different; I am different' at the most palatable end of the difference spectrum, to 'You are evil' at the other end.

This is relevant to the lectionary text for today. Jesus of Nazareth is in the desert and meets with the devil, the embodiment of evil. So much of our lives are spent in turning away from the idea of calling people evil and calling their actions evil instead. So much conflict arises when we face evil behaviour – and, for many of us, the people we call evil because of their evil behaviour. What do we do in light of this? Does Jesus' engagement with the tempter from Matthew's Gospel offer us any insights into the everyday conflicts we find ourselves party to?

Comment

When I was 15, I was part of a summer church festival. It was extraordinary – I met some great friends, went on some exciting adventures, crossed the border multiple times and also found myself able to make some decisions about my religion that felt like my decisions, not the decisions taken for me.

After the camp, I came home with some new friends, some new cross-border experiences, some new devotions and an

extraordinary commitment to seeing the devil every day. I'd
pray at night: reflecting on the day, reading a text and naming
requests for all the people I loved – and then I'd rebuke the
devil. I don't know who told me to do that – it might have been
a practice I'd invented all by myself – but it was extraordinary
how, when I went looking for the devil, I found the devil. Of
course, most of the areas in my life where I found Lucifer were
the areas where I was conflicted: about sex, about jealousies,
about rage I couldn't express. It's more entertaining to rebuke
Satan than reflect on Self. Much of my own spiritual commitment has been nurtured by criticizing overt reliances on devil
diagnosis. And yet, and yet, and yet … we have this week's
text.

Jesus is in the wilderness, and after fasting for 40 days,
he is hungry and is visited by the tempter. This encounter
itself occurs in two gospels – that of Luke and this text from
Matthew; it is referred to only briefly in the Gospel of Mark
(1.12–13) and not at all in John.

The three temptations are interesting. In Luke it goes: Bread /
Mountain / Temple, perhaps because Luke's over-arching concern is 'What will happen when Jesus gets to Jerusalem?'
However, in Matthew's Gospel, the order goes: Bread / Temple
/ Mountain – with a more topographical concern. This journey towards a mountain top also mirrors the literary features
of Moses' journey. At one point it was even thought that the
five sermons of Matthew's Gospel echoed the five books of
the Torah; however, that analysis is a fanciful thing of the
mid-twentieth century. What is interesting, however, is that
Matthew is depicting Jesus' ministry as being pre-figured by a
time of aloneness in the wilderness and a time where Jesus has
to come face to face with something.

It seems too easy to imagine the devil as a character – the
Greek of Matthew's text has him named as *diabolos* and the
peirazo (the tempter) and finally, from the mouth of Jesus
himself, the name Satan (the Adversary) is used – that word
originating in Job's extraordinary poem. The conflict is occurring on a few levels. There is the first and most obvious level:

Jesus is being confronted with something that he might want, namely, bread, power or wealth. Jesus is not without bread, power or finances; the question is what the quality of his relationship with these things will be. Will they have power over him, or will he use bread, power and finance for other purposes? The gospel writer weaves a subtle story for us. The drama of the devil – does he have hooves, horns and fire for his eyes? – masks the fact that the things about which we are tempted are often completely justifiable. Jesus did need sustenance, connection, a sense of his power. Hidden underneath the supernatural image of a tempter appearing to a hungry pilgrim in a desert is a story of how we must all – especially in times of weakness – come into conflict with the reasonable things we desire. It is reasonable to desire to survive, but what values might we compromise as we survive?

Conflict – especially dramatic conflict – can come with such high power that it can be easy to abandon those practices of virtue and justice that we know are most important. This text demonstrates a person at their end who can nonetheless reflect on choices as if he were making them freely, even if he wasn't. He was hungry, making choices about the ethics of how he filled his belly. He was friendless, making choices about how he would conduct his social affairs. He was without influence, making choices about the quality of how he'd wield power.

For us, too. May we – in conflict – have repeated phrases, poems, mantras, prayers that continue to turn us to what will centre us.

Response

Strange as it may seem, it might be interesting for groups of people to talk about their temptations, especially the mild ones. By this, I don't mean to have the equivalent of public confession, but rather to tell everyday stories about a time when you thought about something small and decided to do it – or not do it; what was involved, what returned you to the practice of a virtue that held you.

It could be about a seemingly small lie; or a choice about whether to recycle; or not participating in an event that was exclusionary; or not challenging a pejorative statement; or giving credit; or not giving credit.

So many experiences of distress and conflict could be alleviated if we didn't feel so alone. How can we create hospitality and community in narrating stories of challenge – little and large – in the right kinds of supportive environments?

Prayer

Jesus in the wilderness –
your mouth
must have tasted of sand;
your skin must have been dry
and your body weak.
What kept you steady?
Jesus, keep us steady
in the practice of what is
true and just and beautiful.
Because even hungry, even alone,
even insignificant
you were held steady
by the old prayers
and older words
in your heart.
Jesus, keep us steady.
Amen.

Note

1 Joseph Liechty and Cecelia Clegg, *Moving Beyond Sectarianism: Religion, Conflict and Reconciliation in Northern Ireland*, Dublin: Columba Press, 2000.

Lent 2 – John 3.1–17

Trevor Williams

Introduction

You are listening to a friend who has had a terrible experience. They tell how they have been treated unjustly by someone they had trusted. In hearing their story, you can see why they are hurt, distressed and angry. You feel like having a word with the person whom you think has caused the trouble to put them right. But as you talk with the person who hurt your friend, suddenly you find out there is a whole lot more to the incident than you first realized. Hearing both sides of a story can cause you to change your opinion radically. Do you remember a time when you experienced something like this?

There is something like this going on as Nicodemus meets Jesus. He was a Pharisee, a leader among his people, and Jesus was often in conflict with Nicodemus' fellow Pharisees. Yet there was something about Jesus that intrigued Nicodemus. He comes diffidently, secretly, at night, to get an answer to a question that won't go away.

Comment

John's Gospel tells us that Nicodemus, a Pharisee, was a leader of 'the Jews', a term that John uses – problematically – to denote those who were opposed to Jesus and his teaching. Nicodemus also came by night – light and darkness are key defining themes of this gospel. Here, 'night' denotes opposition to God's reign. In the first 11 chapters of John's Gospel, Jesus meets people in public in the day. Nicodemus comes secretly, at night.

He doesn't come with a question but with a statement: 'No one can do these signs that you do apart from the presence of God.' He recognizes the very essence of God in the signs that Jesus is performing and is intrigued as to what this might mean. Jesus picks up on his phrase 'the presence of God' and responds that 'No one can see the kingdom of God without being born from above'. This too is simply a statement and passes no judgement on Nicodemus. However, Nicodemus' incredulity that a grown person could be 'born again' reveals just how much he remains in the dark. The Greek word *anōthen* can mean 'born again' or 'born from above' or both.[1]

Jesus is drawing the distinction between Nicodemus' objective assessment of the 'signs' within Jesus' ministry as denoting the presence of God and the intriguing invitation to not only observe but to step into the stream of God's activity in the world. Here, 'seeing the reign of God' requires more than right thinking – it is a consequence of a life whose actions are directed and empowered by the Spirit. Nicodemus believed that the presence of God was revealed in Jesus' ministry, but as Jesus points out later in the exchange, 'No one can enter the kingdom of God without being born of water and the Spirit.' The water of baptism is the mark of joining a community. The gift of the Spirit is participating in 'the presence of God' active in the world.

The new life, that of the Spirit, is talked about in this passage in the language of 'action'. Jesus uses the metaphor of wind: 'You don't know where [the wind] comes from or where it goes. So it is with everyone who is born of the Spirit.' As you discern wind because of its effects, says Jesus, so it is with those who are born from above; they are, like Jesus, heralds of the reign of God.

Nicodemus is clearly lost at this point. Jesus uses a rabbinical method of arguing from the lesser (earthly things) to the greater (heavenly things), pointing Nicodemus back to the incident when the Israelites were offered salvation from the plague of vipers by looking at the bronze serpent which Moses lifted up on a 'pole' (Numbers 21.9). We can imagine this pole having a vertical cross bar at the top with a serpent entwined around it. In using this story, Jesus again is forming a 'sign' (the word for 'pole' can also mean 'sign'): 'So must the Son of Man be lifted up, that whoever believes in him may have eternal life.'

'Very truly, I tell you, no one can enter the kingdom of God without being born of water and Spirit.' Jesus' response to Nicodemus' secretive, night-time meeting is a demand that Nicodemus should not just admire Jesus' ministry, or even to state that the signs that Jesus performs demonstrate the presence of God, but that Nicodemus should be baptized, be part of the Jesus community, living life in the guidance and strength of the Spirit.

Response

We are not sure why Nicodemus came to Jesus 'by night'. In what contexts do you find it difficult to be yourself, to stand up for what you believe in? Why is that? Is it right sometimes to be less than open?

There are two other references to Nicodemus in John's Gospel: in the first he gives a somewhat half-hearted defence of Jesus who was in conflict with the religious authorities (7.50–52); the second is when Nicodemus helps Joseph of Arimathea with the burial of Jesus (19.38–42) by providing a super-abundance of spices for the embalming of the body. Was this, at last, Nicodemus moving from darkness to light? In any case, the challenge for Nicodemus, and for us, is not only to 'believe' but, as part of the Christian community, to be signs of the reign of God in the 'night time' world. How is your Christian community being 'light' in the 'night'?

John's usage of 'the Jews' throughout the Fourth Gospel is problematic and has, over the course of centuries, been used to justify anti-Semitism. Has your practice of Christianity been done at the expense of other faith communities? What could you do about this?

Prayer

Jesus Christ,
by your words and deeds, you revealed God's love for
   the world.
Fill with your Spirit the members of your body, the Church,
in our time and in our world
so that we may be good news for those in need,
not only by our words of concern,
but in actions that reflect your love for all.
We ask this for the glory of Jesus Christ.
Amen.

Note

1 W. E. Vine, *Expository Dictionary of New Testament Words* (London: Oliphant, 1978), vol. I, pp. 16, 41.

Lent 3 – John 4.5–42
Pádraig Ó Tuama

Introduction

Conflicts rarely occur in a vacuum. Today's story is a beloved one, told in the inimitable style of the Gospel of John. It's a long dialogue between Jesus and an unnamed Samaritan woman, wherein they speak of faith and blessing and secrets and religion.

However, this story is also a window into a larger reality: the conflicts between Jews and Samaritans, as well as the hinted-at conflict between this woman and her other townspeople. The window of this story opens up a longer, complex reality that incorporates gender, imperial and nationalist powers. A single conflict that occurs between two people sometimes is such a signal: pointing to the old stories that keep recurring again and again.

Comment

'What cannot be remembered', Freud said, 'will be repeated.'[1] For him, this was the way of describing how people recreate unresolved stories from their past in their present and future. Our unconscious, he argues, is trying to process the unprocessed trauma. This can occur in individuals, and national or civic traumas can also be repeated in individual stories. So, an Irish person and a British person – individuals each – might find themselves caught in a story of conflict that mirrors 700 years of British–Irish relations; their interaction opens up a window into something that has not yet been remembered well in the larger stories of their belonging. People find themselves wrapped up – or partially wrapped up – in the stories into which they were born.

This isn't to say that the individual dynamics between two people can be entirely explained by their political realities, but it is to say that sometimes the individual stories are linked to a larger story.

So it is here, with the story of Jesus and this remarkable Samaritan woman, whose name we do not know.

On a narrative level, this is one of the extended dialogues that is so characteristic of John's Gospel (e.g. 3.1–21; 6.22–71; 7.14–52; 8.12–59; 9.1–41;10.22–42). These dialogues are frequently filled with conflict – the conflict of belief/unbelief; of light/dark; of following/not following. John's Gospel has binary themes which he frequently manifests in the escalated engagements that Jesus has. His gospel was 'written that you may believe' and so these dialogues serve to demonstrate what is important to Jesus and – obviously – what the writer of the gospel wishes the reader to grasp. The dialogues serve as a way of embodying the message of Jesus into a tool for the listeners to this gospel to embody in their own lives.

The Samaritan woman is one of the most richly depicted people of this gospel and it is worthwhile noting what a magnificent character she is – she is a person worthy of being imitated. When Jesus speaks to her, she questions his audacity in speaking; when he promises her water that will never run out, she replies that he has no bucket. She is quick witted, undaunted, intelligent, observant and engaging; and the tone of the description and the open heartedness of her language shows her as a person at ease with language, careful about other people's motivations and not ashamed of her needs.

Samaritans, it's thought, were part of a remnant of Jews left behind after the initial conquest of the ten northern tribes of Israel by Assyrians in about the seventh century BCE. Those who stayed behind – or, more accurately, were left behind – intermarried with other peoples. Their Jewish practices became mixed with other religious practices; and while it maintained many of the aspects of Judaism, was distinct enough to cause significant sectarian anxiety between the two belongings. These two religious devotions were not as far apart as some depictions imagine: they did worship on different mountains, yes, but many of the emendations of the Samaritan Torah are what finally ended up in an agreed-upon Torah of Judaism.

So here, representatives of two people are speaking to each other. Their conversation can be seen to begin as representative of their gender identities; then move on to their religious/political identities; before finally getting personal.

The Samaritan woman's surprise that a Jewish man is speaking to her is evident and engaging. She is up for banter, and is brilliant with it, through gender norms and religious conversations. There is, however, a hint of her own possible isolation in the text. She is collecting water at the hottest time of the day. Others from her village would have been there earlier, when it was cooler. Possibly her reputation meant either that she was shunned, or that she avoided the company of people who might shun her. Jesus' invitation for her to call her husband could be seen as an indication that he wishes her to be met with hospitality at the deepest place of her isolation from her community; surely a confronting invitation, and one that can be considered for all readers of religious texts – namely, meet your God in the places you normally hide from.

Of course, there is also a possible national explanation for this: biblical scholar Sandra Schneiders suggests that the five husbands may be a literary device to refer to the infidelities of Samaria in straying and dabbling in false gods.[2] If so, then the reading continues to have deep theological resonances: a shunned person becomes a missionary to her community, giving a vital and salvific message to people who would seem to rather avoid her company.

Whether she is a symbol for her people or a historical person in her own right, a message remains: remember yourself in a new way so that you do not need to repeat and project your past compulsively, but rather re-member the story of yourself into a new form of freedom and belonging. This is at the heart of being a person of peace, a person who can be fully present – with insight, humour, intuition and spontaneity – in conflicts.

Response

For private reflection: how might current, difficult relationships be understood as a window into something that needs to be remembered in a new way so that the past does not keep repeating itself?

What role can vulnerability, spontaneity, freedom and conversation have in this imaginative re-membering?

Prayer

Thirsty Jesus,
you sat by a well and instead of reaching in yourself
created community with someone who came seeking solitude.
In all our solitudes, meet us,
especially in the solitudes where we cannot recognize
how we are repeating the same dry story.
Because yours is the water
that refreshes dry stories
so that they may spring up
with new life
and give life to many.
Amen.

Notes

1 See Adam Phillips, *Becoming Freud* (New Haven, CT: Yale University Press, 2016).

2 See Sandra Schneiders, *Written That You May Believe*, 2nd edn (Chicago, IL: Independent Publishers Group, 2003).

Lent 4 – John 9.1–41

Pádraig Ó Tuama

Introduction

This long gospel reading about a man born blind is rich in interpersonal dynamics, readings of how 'us' and 'them' dynamics play out, readings about limiting questions and readings about disability.

The disciples' question assumes that sin was the cause of the man's blindness and this question of 'causality' continues to invade the lives of many people. While Jesus elevates the answer somewhat, it is true that the gospels in general treat blindness as a metaphor. I once asked a Corrymeela Community member, Dave, who is blind what he thinks about this idea of blindness as a metaphor for lack of insight. He said, 'Don't use my impairment as a metaphor for your ignorance.' It's a wise point he makes.

We see in this text the struggle to believe. So many of the characters are unable to believe what they so plainly see in front of them. It can be a fearful thing to not be believed, because you risk expulsion, like the parents in this narrative. And subsequently, harsh borders between who is in the 'us' crowd and who is in the 'them' crowd can be established, to the detriment of belief, community and transformation.

In situations of conflict, questions, definitions of 'us' and the tendency to disbelieve what you do not understand are all severe limitations upon friendship, connection and belonging. Such dynamics are artfully outlined here by John.

Comment

In the first instance, this text may be summarized in a series of questions.

- 'Rabbi, who sinned, this man or his parents, that he was born blind?'
- 'Is this not the man who used to sit and beg?'
- But they kept asking him, 'Then how were your eyes opened?'
- They said to him, 'Where is he?' He said, 'I do not know.'
- Some of the Pharisees said, 'This man is not from God, for he does not observe the sabbath.' But others said, 'How can a man who is a sinner perform such signs?'
- And they were divided. So they said again to the blind man, 'What do you say about him? It was your eyes he opened.' He said, 'He is a prophet.'
- 'Is this your son, who you say was born blind? How then does he now see?'
- 'We know that this is our son, and that he was born blind; but we do not know how it is that now he sees, nor do we know who opened his eyes. Ask him; he is of age. He will speak for himself.'
- They said to him, 'What did he do to you? How did he open your eyes?'
- He answered them, 'I have told you already, and you would not listen. Why do you want to hear it again? Do you also want to become his disciples?'
- They answered him, 'You were born entirely in sins, and are you trying to teach us?' And they drove him out.
- 'Do you believe in the Son of Man?'
- He answered, 'And who is he, sir?'
- Some of the Pharisees near him heard this and said to him, 'Surely we are not blind, are we?'

Taking this summary approach, one can see questions that display curiosity, invitation, constriction and hostility. The binary question 'Who sinned? This man or his parents?' allows no space whatsoever for questioning, 'Why are you asking about sin?' The lens through which the disciples view the life of the man born blind from birth is so limiting and it is they, in the first instance, who are in need of intellectual, social and moral conversion. Sometimes it is the mode of questioning, and the background thinking that leads to the question, that contribute to situations of conflict.

Where the disciples were constrained into a question of assigning sin, the Pharisees are likewise constrained into siloed camps of 'us' and 'them'. It is interesting to pay attention to some of the pronouns (we, you, he, they, I) in the questions and surrounding dialogue:

- So for the second time *they* called the man who had been blind, and *they* said to *him*, 'Give glory to God! *We* know that this man is a sinner.'
- *He* answered *them*, '*I* have told *you* already, and *you* would not listen. Why do *you* want to hear it again? Do *you* also want to become his disciples?'
- Then *they* reviled *him*, saying, '*You* are his disciple, but *we* are disciples of Moses. *We* know that God has spoken to Moses, but as for this man, *we* do not know where *he* comes from.'
- The man answered, 'Here is an astonishing thing! *You* do not know where *he* comes from, and yet *he* opened my eyes. *We* know that God does not listen to sinners, but *he* does listen to one who worships *him* and obeys *his* will. Never since the world began has it been heard that anyone opened the eyes of a person born blind. If this man were not from God, *he* could do nothing.'
- *They* answered him, '*You* were born entirely in sins, and are *you* trying to teach *us*?' And *they* drove him out.
- Some of the Pharisees near *him* heard this and said to *him*, 'Surely *we* are not blind, are *we*?' Jesus said to *them*, 'If *you* were blind, *you* would not have sin. But now that *you* say, "*We* see," your sin remains.'

One can see how language that causes delineation between people and language that invites is evident in these dialogues. The blind man uses 'we' in a way to seek to build bridges, building on his own dramatic experience of sight. In response, he, by association, is in turns both disbelieved and then expelled. The man born blind seeks to gather, but the response seeks to expel. The man's parents seek to avoid this peril by advising the Pharisees to speak to their son directly.

And so we see the complicated interface between simple concepts that are at the heart of all human gatherings: the quality of the questions we ask, the way we formulate our questions and the way in which we talk about belonging.

At the heart of the whole text is a man whose story is not believed. People deny that he is who he is; that he has experienced what he has experienced; that he is telling the truth. He is, in his body and self, the site of controversy. He is responding to the full truth that he knows, and in turn he is treated in a way that becomes the shibboleth of true orthodoxy.

It is a recipe for scapegoating and exclusion. It is also a recipe for the abdication of responsibility and self-reflection. Such dynamics can be at the heart of every human gathering – especially among creative, dynamic, well-intentioned gatherings of people. How a group respond to an individual whose life or circumstances or narrative challenges the group's belonging or viewpoint is a test of the integrity of the group's belonging.

Response

In groups, it may be worthwhile paying attention to articles in various news sites that make use of the plural pronouns: us, we, they, them, their. What theology is being presented here? How can we increase scrutiny of our own usage of such terms, especially where they build suspicion rather than open curiosity?

Prayer

God of groups,
you are within and beyond all of our borders:
our names for you; our words about you; our gatherings
   and stories.
We seek to praise but sometimes we imprison.
May we always be curious about what is beyond our borders,
going there gently, knowing you have always been there.
We ask this because we know that you are within and beyond
   all of our stories.
Amen.

Lent 5 – John 11.1–45

Pádraig Ó Tuama

Introduction

We speak about conflicts within ourselves and also conflicts between individuals and communities. However, it is also true to recognize that conflict can be part of the human condition. Conflict can be the source of art and ache. Conflict can be the source of change and human transformation. It can be what calls us into our deepest yearning and our greatest endeavour.

The text for this week, from the Gospel of John (and towards the end of what theologians call John's first 12 chapters, 'The Book of Signs'), brings us some of the great themes of humanity: misunderstanding, grief, death, emotion, change, risk.

One can approach this particular text as part of the Christological depiction of Jesus of Nazareth through the writings of the Fourth Gospel. One can also approach it, as we will do in this reflection, as a narrative that gathers in some of the existential crises of being human. How are we when we are in pain? How can we understand ourselves and each other? We so often misunderstand each other and are unsure what to do. In our bodies, we are sites of great desire and emotion. The Jesus of John's Gospel, it is true, arrives on the scene a fully developed person, conscious and confident of his mission and identity as the Son of God. However, the Jesus of John is also depicted as a man of emotion, a man who loved his friends, and upon whom his friends depended and called – as Mary and Martha do when their brother Lazarus is on the brink of death.

Comment

One of the themes in John's Gospel is that of misunderstanding. We see it from the first miracle at the wedding of Cana. The servants have served the pitchers of water-become-wine and the understanding is that the host of the wedding has broken convention and served fine wine later rather than earlier. One of the writer's techniques is to present events that have multiple interpretations – the immediate and the underneath. While many of the characters respond to the immediate interpretation, the invitation to the reader is to perceive and respond to the deeper meaning.

The theme of misunderstanding can be seen in Jesus' discussion with Nicodemus, who asks, 'How can I be born again?' and in the engaging dialogue between Jesus and the Samaritan woman who, when in conversation about water of life, says, 'Sir, you have no bucket.' This literary technique of misunderstanding continues and, in a certain sense, reaches a culmination in the eleventh chapter with the story of Jesus, Mary, Martha and Lazarus.

It is in this chapter, with its many layers of misunderstanding, that the reader feels as if they are one of the characters in the text. Why did Jesus delay? Why did he go into hostile territory? Why the protracted conversation with Martha, herself in the grip of grief? Why did he weep at the grave? The onlookers in the text have one interpretation of Jesus' tears and readers have produced many more over centuries. And perhaps one of the greatest curiosities of the text is about Lazarus. What happened to him after he had the grave clothes removed? How did he live again and how did he die again? How did the siblings of Bethany understand this strange miracle and the tears of their friend Jesus?

In John's Gospel, a link can be established between a 'sign' and the ensuing discussion about the significance of that sign, followed then by a discourse about Jesus' identity and purpose. This can be seen in how Jesus as the 'bread of life' (6.35, 41, 48, 51), as the 'light of the world' (8.12), as the 'good shepherd' (10.7, 9) and finally as 'life' (11.25), is the perplexing identity story that leads to discussions and misunderstandings and irony and perceptions in the chapters that follow each of these phrases. However, these stories also demonstrate the conflict and complexity of understanding what it meant to follow Jesus in the settings of the day and can highlight a story of faith that feels very appropriate for readers today.

It can be difficult to know how to pray, and it can be difficult to know what to do when prayers as sincere as those of Mary and Martha go unanswered. It can be hard to know what it is that moves God, even when we are moved in our own circumstances or prayer.

In Mary and Martha, in Lazarus and the disciples, we find companions on the road where friendship with Jesus is accompanied by bewilderment. What did he mean? How did he make his decisions? How do we follow? How do we understand? How do we make sense of what he does? And how do we continue in the midst of misunderstanding? In John's Gospel we see that while the reader is invited to perceive the deeper meaning of Jesus' glory – an aspect of his identity that is divine and therefore mysterious and difficult to understand – the reader is also invited to see Jesus as a friend: he cleans his friends' feet; visits their homes; and he says, 'Greater love has no one than to give their life for their friends.' The project of perception is accompanied by the faithfulness of friendship.

In our own prayer, with its bewilderments and conflicts, benefits and constraints, we may recognize that true understanding is a goal that evades us. However, understanding is only one outcome. Friendship, faithfulness, accompaniment, solidarity and shared stories of life – however bewildering – is another set of outcomes that are possible, no matter how evasive deep meanings are in the unpredictable circumstances of life.

Response

One of the things I most value about John's Gospel is that while the picture of Jesus in it is most comprehensively one of a Christ – The Word, who is to be Believed – it is also one that depicts him as emotional and with deep love for his friends. This brings us to the strange reality that most of our friendships probably oscillate between mystery and understanding, complication and affection, misunderstanding and accompaniment.

What are the friendships in your life that hold that space between these contrasting states of being?

Prayer

God of all time,
we ask, we weep, we wait, we die, we hope, we live,
we carry on, we pick ourselves up, we try to understand,
we misunderstand, we learn, we ask again,
we wait for understanding.
In all of these, may prayer be a companion, not a torment.
May we find in prayer the consolation
that sustains us through all things,
knowing that some things change,
and some things remain the same.
Amen.

Lent 6 Liturgy of the Palms – Matthew 21.1–11

Pádraig Ó Tuama

Introduction

Greta Thunberg's school strike was a humble action which has now spread around the world. It is perhaps not too much of an exaggeration to say it has changed the world, offered a new form of protest for young people and attracted considerable criticism from world leaders.

It can sometimes be instructive to think about those times when you have exercised authority – especially if you have tried to do so in a quiet or humble way – and to reflect on how effective that action was and about how much conflict it may have given rise to.

Comment

Jesus has arrived in Jerusalem.

This is such a well-known story that it can be easy to miss both the artistry and the intensity of the event. For Matthew – and for Luke and Mark – Jesus only comes to Jerusalem once. Matthew and Luke have their birth stories; then some narratives about being launched into ministry (usually with a story of temptation); then the ministry of healing and freedom around Galilee; all with the eyes set to when Jesus would arrive in Jerusalem. Jesus' engagements with religious and imperial authorities raises curiosity and speculation during the Galilee ministry, but it's totally understood that if Jesus ever went to Jerusalem that all hell might break loose.

In an artistic sense, it is a classic hero narrative: there is a hero, with a message and/or a purpose; the hero is raising a reputation by doing some work; all the while people are wondering, 'What's going to happen when the Hero gets to the City?' It may not be a city, it might be Mordor, or a showdown with Voldemort, or Oz, or a hundred other locations where the new power of the hero confronts the established power.

Matthew, Mark and Luke's Gospels all hinge on this, and many people do not know that the synoptic gospels do not portray Jesus entering and leaving Jerusalem throughout his ministry. It is only John's Gospel – which has a very different narrative structure – that depicts Jesus in and out of Jerusalem throughout the three years of his public ministry.

Matthew's Jesus has been building up a reputation – in word and deed – and is now arriving in a place of conflict, a place where his bold message – a radical reading of an ancient covenant – will directly challenge both those who are in current religious authority as well as the imperial force who are in political and national authority. Authority of one clashes with the authority of others.

Jesus enters humbly – this adjective is so important in the text – on the back of an animal and is given a welcome of two stories: the welcome of a king, but the welcome of a humble king, sitting, as the prophets had dreamed, on the back of a work animal. This is no entry on a stallion, but a depiction of a way of undoing, reframing, de-escalating an expected conflict. Jesus' approach to this great city is in the name of a demure demonstration of his mass appeal, but it has the opposite effect – it escalates rather than de-escalates the tension.

There is a detail in this text that has perturbed readers for centuries. The disciples are told to get two animals – a donkey and a colt – 'They brought the donkey and the colt, and put their cloaks on them, and he sat on them.' What did Jesus sit on, though? The donkey? The colt? Could he have sat on both at the same time? Did he swap halfway through the triumphal entry? Ancient scholars saw that one of the animals represented Jews and the other represented Gentiles. Calvin was the first to recognize the usage of a literary device whereby a singular is spoken of in the plural in order to place emphasis on the singular. This literary technique rejoices in the easily remembered term *parallelismus membrorum*.

Literary devices aside, the depiction of Jesus' humble arrival is the point. His humility is the very thing that astounds the people, deepens their attention towards him and attracts aggression from those who see that their positions, roles and authority are going to be undermined by this new attention towards a Galilean upstart. In the Gospel of Matthew, Jesus seems fully aware of this. He requisitions animals like a monarch would, his arrival draws high drama and he seems to know that he is on his way to his death. The escalating conflict that many are expecting – and perhaps even eagerly expecting – is undone by his refusal to command his followers to take up arms.

Humble – *praus* in Greek – can also be translated as meek, kind, benevolent, gentle, forgiving. This, and particularly this, seems to be a significant point of disruption to the expected narrative of conflict in Jerusalem. Jesus arrives, and a power-off is expected, but the approach taken is one of humility, meekness, kindness, benevolence, gentleness and forgiveness. Jesus is no wallflower – he is confident in his critique, but his power is used to gather in those who have been dispossessed, rather than to incite revolution.

Taking this approach towards expected conflicts in Jerusalem did not mean that Jesus avoided conflict; indeed in this case, it escalated it. But it meant that he maintained his own integrity in the conflict. The escalation did not cause him to lose control of the conflict values that mattered most. This cost him his life but, for him, this was a price worth paying.

Response

It might be an interesting thing to seek out examples – from the news, or from local stories – of people using humility in their approach to expected conflicts. Obviously, it's always easy to find those who enjoy escalating conflicts, but contemporary examples of humility would be interesting.

Such examples will, despite their humility, cause debate: just because someone adopts a manner that's subversive and mild, it doesn't mean all – or even many – will agree with their aims. But this will be even more informative. Jesus, too, had large appeal, but caused deep division.

Prayer

Humble Jesus,
you arrived into a city like a peasant and a king
and lit a fuse that you knew was waiting for a light.
And it didn't save you from anything.
When we walk into conflict,
help us find the approach that's true.
Not because it'll give surety
but because it has integrity.
Just like you.
Amen.

Lent Year B – 'Private and Public'

The reflections for Lent Year B form a thematic set which invites us to focus our attention on the figure of Jesus and to explore the conversations and tensions between the private and the public as we see him wrestling with these in his own life and ministry.

Introduction to the Set

Pádraig Ó Tuama

Lent has six Sundays, including Palm Sunday. The readings are introduced on Ash Wednesday with imperatives: 'Beware of practising your piety before others in order to be seen by them,' Matthew's Jesus warns. The remaining six Sundays of Lent bring the voices of Mark's Jesus and John's Jesus to us:

- We revisit the baptism and wilderness experiences of Jesus from Mark.
- The second Sunday brings us Mark's narration of the Transfiguration.
- The third Sunday of Lent moves to John's account of Jesus' clearing of the temple.
- The fourth Sunday stays with John and the first Nicodemus passage.
- The fifth Sunday of Lent has us hearing Jesus' words about a grain of wheat dying, from the beginning of the 'Book of Glory' in John.
- The final Sunday in Lent – Palm Sunday – we rejoin Mark for his account of the grand entrance to Jerusalem.

So we can see a form of journey through this sombre springtime. It is a time to pay attention, to be rooted in the foundation of calling and to hold what is most important in front of us, in order to remove trinkets and temptations, to use the mind, to love – even when it makes demands – and to follow, even to unknown ends.

Let us read and let us follow together. As these reflections are being written, the world is hunkering down to stop the spread of the virus; so, let us find nurture in the dark earth of these texts, letting the heart be strengthened by the stories of one man at the corner of an empire who challenged empire.

Ash Wednesday – Matthew 6.1–6, 16–21

Pádraig Ó Tuama

Introduction

Lent, it is good to remember, comes from the word for spring. *Lento* we hear, and Vivaldi's springtime music makes daffodils emerge among us. Other languages render this season before Easter with different imaginations – Irish, for instance, calls Lent *carghas*, deriving from the Latin word for 40.

In a time of pandemic, and with the world marking a year since most places went into forms of lockdown, or distancing, or caution, or mourning, it may be good to remind ourselves of the springtime at the heart of Lent. That is true whatever hemisphere we are in: whether our seasons are moving from winter to spring; or from summer into autumn, or from dry to rainy, it is good to keep *Lento* at the heart of this Lent.

Comment

The text for Ash Wednesday's reading is a sombre one, filled with imperatives:

- Beware
- Do not sound a trumpet
- Do not let your left hand know what your right hand is doing
- Do not be like the hypocrites when you pray. Go into your room
- Shut the door
- Pray to your Father who is in secret. Do not look dismal
- Put oil on your head
- Wash your face

These are familiar words for people familiar with Lent. But familiarity can cause us to recognize rather than read the words. This Ash Wednesday, order is less a critique of self-proclamation (although, to be sure, it is that too), and more an invitation into secrecy.

Five times the Gospel of Matthew uses the word secret and four of those instances are in this text:

- 'so that your alms may be done in secret; and your Father who sees in secret will reward you.'
- 'But whenever you pray, go into your room and shut the door and pray to your Father who is in secret; and your Father who sees in secret will reward you.'

Secret, secret, secret, secret.

The word secret in the Greek of the gospels is *kruptos*, meaning hidden or concealed. *Kruptos*, as can be heard, is the origin of the word crypt in today's English, as well as cryptocurrency. The word entered Italian, too, giving way to grotto, meaning a little cave, familiar perhaps to those whose religious traditions have grottos with images of the mother of God.

So Ash Wednesday, and by association Lententide, is an invitation to a certain kind of secrecy, of concealment. Like tulip bulbs beginning to move in the deep earth, the hope of life that is at the heart of Eastertide is to be held during a time of sobriety.

What will help us keep this time? A little less display and a little more reflection. It's not easy to do with children at home to homeschool, with worry about the roll-outs of vaccines, with anxiety about infections, with concern about employment. Lent is not a time to burden the burdened. Lent is finding a way to pay attention to small springtimes that will nurture. It is, ultimately, finding a way to let attention to love be given attention. It might just take a moment – the length of time it takes to wait for the kettle to boil, the length of time it takes to look at the sunrise in the morning, the length of time it takes to say yes to the prayer that our lives will become safer as the year moves through. It can be a breath, that's all that's needed; one breath after the other.

Lent is less about that discipline you chose – giving up chocolate, or wine, or caffeine – and more about the time you make for giving attention to the unseen thing that holds you together. It might be reading a poem. It is less about displays of piety and more about making time to make that donation to a cause you admire. It is less about less and more about more. More attention to the dark earth that nurtures us, rather than the dramas that demean us. Conflict, week on week, is exhausting. Lent is an invitation into a certain deliberate form of rest from the noise that maddens us. I love the news, I love politics, I love ideas. So I'll keep listening to the headlines, but this Lent I'll turn the radio off after the headlines. There are other conversations I need to listen to for 40 days.

Happy Lenten Springtime, wherever we find ourselves in the world. Happy secrecy. Happy focus.

Prayer

Buried bulb,
stirring a little in the earth.
Turning, too, with shoots of green
feeding in the dark.

Spring up around us
during Lenten noise and quietude,
and in us too.

So that we might be given life
by what is life-giving beneath our feet;
so that we might give life
to secret things
nurtured in the quiet places of our desire.
Amen.

Lent 1 – Mark 1.9–15

Pádraig Ó Tuama

Introduction

In today's gospel – a text of just 130 words – we hear Mark's introduction of Jesus; his baptism by John in the Jordan and the voice coming from heaven; the temptation in the wilderness; the arrest of John; and the beginning of Jesus' proclamation of good news. This is the breathtaking pace of the Gospel of Mark.

And yet, in the midst of the frenetic pace of Mark's narration, there is a call to quietude. A voice of love and affirmation comes for Jesus, during a time when public attention towards figures of critique is high, and Jesus is driven. Not driven in reputation (although he's not frightened of reputation) but rather driven into a necessary wilderness, to take account of the words spoken to him, to face his own temptations and to find comfort both in prayer and the earth.

Even as you read this, listen to yourself as you take a breath. Time passes the way time passes. Some things feel frenetic. Even in pressured time, there is the possibility of listening to the sound of your breath in your body.

Comment

We are back to the start of Mark's Gospel for this reading, and the only mention of the temptation in the desert that this Lent offers.

In Matthew and Luke's Gospels, Jesus of Nazareth's engagement with the Satan in the wilderness is a significant narrative replete with details. Here, however, it is covered with Mark's characteristic breathtaking speed. The Spirit drives Jesus out into the wilderness where he remains for 40 days, tempted by the Satan; keeping the company of wild beasts and angels. Boom.

This temptation is squeezed between Jesus' baptism and John's arrest. The former (accompanied by the heavenly voice of affirming love) is the narrative precursor to the wilderness time; and the arrest is the narrative precursor to Jesus' public ministry.

The public affirmation of chosenness drove Jesus to solitude. The public demonstration of corruption drove Jesus to action.

In a way, it's a lesson to live by: in a time when his reputation was being affirmed, Jesus needed time to ground himself. It was – in Mark's schema anyway – the corruption and injustice of an innocent man being arrested (and later executed) that drove Jesus to speak in public. 'Repent,' he says, meaning, 'Change your mind, change your behaviour, change your direction.'

In these short verses, we see Jesus of Nazareth as a character who takes reputation seriously. When he is being lauded, he enters secrecy; when people are being arrested, he raises his voice. This sets up a prototype for the rest of Mark's Gospel, namely that Jesus oscillates between intervention and discretion. The Messianic Secret, it's called – Jesus' strange reluctance to speak about himself in Mark's Gospel. Devils and demons proclaim his identity as God's chosen one and he silences them. Even the Voice of God comes from the heavens and Jesus goes to the desert. Theological and Christological tomes have been written, but sometimes I wonder if it would be better understood through the lens of psychology: Mark's Jesus understood that his life flourished when public attention was matched by private intention.

In an era when many people seek 15 minutes of fame, and some are famous for being famous, it is worthwhile considering the conflicted nature of Jesus' relationship with reputation in this, the earliest of the gospels. Mark's depiction stands in stark contrast to the characterization of Jesus in John's Gospel where, through a succession of 'I am' statements, Jesus names himself in increasingly audacious terms, culminating in his stating 'I am the Life' at Lazarus' graveside – a statement that prompted his detractors to plot his execution. Here though, in this short and fast-paced gospel, we see a different depiction of Jesus.

There is much wisdom in the Marcan depiction of Jesus' caution about reputation. He takes quietude in response to recognition. The recognition, in this case, comes from the Voice of God. So the recognition is not false. Jesus, however, takes time alone in response to it. What is this time alone for? To let the message sink deeper, it seems; but also to consider who he should be in light of these words. He has company in this wilderness: that of temptation, of angels and of wild beasts. In a way, this could be characterized as an inner voice, the experience of the earth and the consolation of prayer.

'What's it like to be you?' the five-year-old daughter of a colleague once asked me. She thought deeply about matters and was asking everyone this question. It seems like she had recently come into a particular awareness of her own person-hood – and that of others – and she wanted to hear the answer to this most personal of questions. I think that Jesus was ask-ing himself a similar question – 'What's it like to be me?' – and he needed space for this complicated, conflicting, creative question.

Nobody can do this work for us. It is work we can only do for ourselves. Loving voices will speak loving things to us (we hope), but even those are not the final word. The invitation from this week's gospel text is to an inner life, an inner life that can listen to its own complexities and conflicts, shoring up wisdom, humility and determination, from which our small works of love and justice can emerge.

Response

One of the interesting features of this week's text is 'and he was with the wild beasts'. It is possible that this strange part of the story was written specifically for early Christians who were facing persecution in arenas with wild animals while spectators cheered (though this was not nearly so widespread as some accounts would have us believe).

Alongside that explanation, I'd like to also offer another one: in the wake of hearing that he had divine purpose, Jesus went to be with other animals. Animals know their own hungers, they forage, they find daily sustenance, they sleep where they sleep and live with caution, as predators may be around any corner. There is a wisdom that comes from watching the other animals with whom we share the planet.

So, as a response – consider animals. You may live with some. As I write this, it is snowing outside. In a few hours I will go and walk some paths to see the tracks of hares and foxes and deer and pleasant pheasants. There are documentaries to watch filled with insight. In this first Sunday of Lent, let us watch the other animals. What do we see? What do they see back?

Prayer

Jesus of the wilderness,
in a time of heightened tensions
you were driven to the wild:
desolate lands with beasts,
temptations and dreams of angels.

In all the tensions of our day
may we find small moments of reflection
to guide us through this Lententide.

May the tracks of the hare remind us
of the wisdom of the hare:
be quick, watch out, don't forget to eat.

May our work for justice be nurtured
by the focus found in wilderness.

We ask this because you asked this, you
needed this; so do we.
Amen.

Lent 2 – Mark 9.2–9

Pádraig Ó Tuama

Introduction

Our readings for the second Sunday in Lent bring us to the Transfiguration and the inner life of Jesus being communicated for his friends to see. He is with Moses and Elijah, symbols of the Law and the Prophets. Peter, one of the friends, wishes this moment would go on for ever. We too – in certain moments of elevation – wish for an experience to last. But – as we know – it doesn't. And so we are brought into the conflict of living with moments of insight alongside the everyday humdrum of our lives and responsibilities.

As we prepare to reflect on the text, it may be worthwhile to remember a fleeting moment of sheer delight. Of course, it did not last for ever, but the experience of it, for however long it lasted, was a gift nonetheless, a gift that is providing nurture far beyond its original duration.

Comment

As a broad breakdown of the structure of the Gospel of Mark, we can highlight:

1: a prologue (1.1–13)
    2: followed by the Galilean ministry (1.14—8.30)
        3: leading to the journey to Jerusalem (8.31—10.52)
      4: the events of Jerusalem, including the last supper and crucifixion (11.1—15.47)
    5: finishing with the details of the tomb (16.1–8, 9–20)

The first and fifth sections echo each other in certain themes of isolation. The second and fourth sections also echo each other in terms of considerations about the disciples.

Section 3 – the central section – is an extraordinary one in which imaginations about the perception of who Jesus is come to the fore. There are stories (problematic because of their uncritical usage of disability as metaphor) about blind people coming to see, and there are harsh statements from Jesus about what it means to follow him; it is also in this section that we find the story of the Transfiguration.

This brief outline of the structure of the story within which Mark's account of the Transfiguration occurs is helpful because it demonstrates the importance of this revelation of Jesus' identity in this particularly secretive of gospels. As we've explored in the previous weeks, the Gospel of Mark, and especially these texts for Lent, consider the relationship of the private life to the public life. The public life is negotiated not only by the individual person – Jesus can decide how he wishes to be in his public statements – but also by the weight of expectation, demand, political and religious burdens which are put on someone in their public witness.

While we are thinking of this in terms of the life of Jesus of Nazareth, we can also extend it to the experience of many people with a public role today: clergy, therapists, chaplains, medics, social workers, teachers, etc. When the identity of your vocation or role or work is known, you can sometimes be perceived as public property, where your expertise can be called upon and where you can be blamed for things even while you are trying to go about your normal business. This tension of how to live your life in public, and how to live with the public perception of your public life, is something that some people with particular roles or calls in society face on a daily basis. Even deeper than roles, sometimes identities, like that of parent or designated carer within a family, can bring with them the complexity of coping with others' expectation of your performance. This has been all the more exacerbated during Covid-19.

In the exhaustion of our roles, we can look for relief, and perhaps hope that the moments of relief can be sufficient.

As Jesus is transfigured, Moses (an embodiment of the Law) and Elijah (an embodiment of the prophets) appear: Jesus is being revealed in light of word and insight. Was this a moment where the gospel writers were portraying Jesus as being in need of support, or recalibration, or reminding? It is near the point where Jesus reaches Jerusalem where – even the dogs know – he will face the brutality of empire. However, Peter interprets the event differently. He is witnessing what he's witnessing and he wishes to remain there.

Peter's outburst is easy to caricature. But in many ways, we can sympathize too: he is enjoying an experience that is elevated from the humdrum of misperception, of vague wondering – he is being given a glimpse into certitude and he does not wish this certitude to be only momentary. He wishes to stay, or perhaps that the moment would stretch on for ever. 'Let us make three dwellings.' He isn't interested in a dwelling for himself or the other disciples – he seems happy for all of them to rough it. He does want to find a way to capture the experience, contain it, perhaps even chain it.

And this is the way with so many of us on the path towards flourishing, whether flourishing in ourselves, our relationships, our work or our spirituality. We have momentary glimpses into something of great beatitude and we wish it could always be like this. Then we go down the mountain and our glimpse seems to fragment; the aftermath can make us wonder if the elevated experience was hollow because of its limitation in time.

This can result in an experience of conflict within ourselves and can cause dis-ease in us. While that discomfort is understandable, it may be possible to take some comfort from it: that life is built on moments of perception mixed alongside moments of misperception; that we can find comfort in the strong memory of elevated moments of prayer, or synchronicity, or creativity, or collaboration, or harmony with loved ones ... and then there's the accompanying everydayness of the times when things just plod along. These two ways of being human are not in conflict with each other; rather, they are part of the experience of an ordinary life.

The wisdom of this text is that a gift of an experience was needed and that Peter's desire for permanence was not met. The moment passes. Jesus and his friends are brought back to the here-and-now, they move to travel down the mountain where challenges await. There are complexities, things that are difficult to understand, questions to ask, things to learn unfolding in front of them. The work of a day. And hopefully some rest, eventually.

Prayer

Transfigured Jesus
you trusted your friends to see a glimpse
of who you knew yourself to be
and this glimpse was momentary.

We see glimpses of who we can be,
of who our communities can be,
of what our art could be, of what our loves could be.
And then we blink and the glimpses seem gone.

Help us be nurtured by these fragmentary perceptions
of possibility. Help us take courage
from tiny reminders of what love can look like.

Especially when we're tired, or feeling far
from such experiences.

Because you had moments of beatitude
that were good enough to carry you through
weeks of trundling toward Jerusalem
toward a clash with powers that sought to undo you.
Amen.

Lent 3 – John 2.13–22

Pádraig Ó Tuama

Introduction

We continue in our reflections on the images of the private and public life of Jesus. In this week's text – the explosive event where the moneylenders and vendors are driven from the temple – we see Jesus in public.

Preparation

There are various theological considerations about this week's gospel reading, and the reflection below will consider one of them. However, by way of preparation, it may be useful to think of a time when you were consumed with zeal; or perhaps anger may be the word for it.

What is your memory of that time? Where in your body did you feel the anger? What did you do with it? As you reflect on it, what are your feelings and analyses? Are you drawn first to the people who were near you, or justification, or regret, or something else?

And then consider the thing that sparked your anger. What was so important to you that you got angry and showed that anger in public? Is that something you're happy with? Or something you're working to change? Would your reflection now be to get less angry in the future? Or to get more angry?

It is always worth saying this, too: tell someone the story of your anger. It might be someone you know well; it might be someone outside of the circumstance; it might be a professional; it might be a neighbour. Telling the story can help us to live with the story and – we hope – learn from the story, so that what is most important can be made manifest.

Comment

Matthew, Mark and Luke place the clearing of the temple in and around the events contributing to Jesus' arrest, whereas John places it at the beginning of Jesus' public life. John's telling of Jesus' public ministry takes place over three successive years, whereas the synoptic gospels can be read as narrating Jesus' public life as if it were all over one year.

The Jesus of John is very clear about his identity and this gospel account has the highest Christology among the four. This Jesus is often in great contrast to the Jesus of Mark, whose public life is defined by a certain secrecy. Nowhere in John, for instance, do we hear Jesus healing people but swearing them to secrecy, a feature that is consistent – although ineffective – in Mark.

Today we hear of Jesus being public – being disruptive – in the place of prayer. It is for this reason, often, that I think Jesus would not have been interested in being a conflict mediator. He didn't spend his ministry trying to stop or mediate conflicts and seemed comfortable in raising them when it seemed important.

The section of the temple where it seems this market was taking place was the Court of the Gentiles. This was the place where Gentiles, women and anyone deemed temporarily – or permanently – unclean could come. Many of them could go no further, so this court would be the fullness of their experience of the temple. And this place was turned from a place of embrace into a place of economics.

To be unclean was often synonymous with being poor – purchasing an animal for a cleansing ritual required money. Hence this court would have been a place where the faithful who couldn't afford to participate in the rituals would have come. In many places, it was a gathering place for all, because all – at one point or another – would have recognized their ritual uncleanliness.

While there was another court for women, there were limits to how far a woman – however ritually pure – could go. The

Court of the Gentiles seems to have been the place where the greatest number of people could pass through. Rather than being seen merely as the first rung in the steps towards the mercy of God, what Jesus seems to be proposing throughout his work is that this Court of the Gentiles is the very place to meet God: in among the hubbub of mixed community, in among the places where you'll meet foreigners and locals, where the clean and unclean intermingle, where women are as present as men. There – in the theological and political and civic imagination of Jesus – is where you'll find God.

And it has been turned into a marketplace. This Court for the All has become a place to burden the burdened, to extort the already excluded. This is the house of God, the house of presence, the house of prayer. No wonder Jesus is enraged.

Often, in positions of conflict, a narrative of faith might urge a quiet path, a reconciliatory path, a path of mediation, of not-making-a-fuss. While that might sometimes be true, it is not always true. In this important text, we see Jesus making a point. And he is not afraid to raise hell with the conflict he creates. Neither should we be.

Turning tables over for the sake of turning tables over is never the point. We know this. The point is to make the point. Often, this can be done by finding campaigns that you believe in and finding out what can actually help: is it promoting a particular person who is speaking for a cause? Is it amplifying their voice? Is it giving some money to a cause that's making a case for a change in policy? Is it supporting a court case where a small agency is suing a large corporation in the name of greater accountability?

Knowing the right way to support an important cause isn't always easy. Sometimes, people can step in claiming to be 'the Voice of the Voiceless' when, in fact, the problem isn't that people are voiceless, it's that people aren't listening. Well-meaning supporters charging in to crowd the chorus of voices isn't going to help. 'What She Said' is a helpful thing to remember: that is, looking for the voices already speaking out and doing what you can to point towards and amplify their voices.

For me, writers like Arundhati Roy, Binyavanga Wainaina, Ta-Nehisi Coates, Rebecca Solnit, Fintan O'Toole and Roxane Gay are contemporary (or, in the case of Binyavanga Wainaina, recently deceased) examples of helpful artistic and social critics: their essays and editorials point beyond the outrage to the underlying facts that should have us turning over tables – not for the sake of turning over tables, but for making a point.

Response

So for a response, some questions: Whose voice do you turn to to bring you deeper into analysis? Whose voice do you amplify because they have the authentic insight and experience to represent the cause they are raising awareness about? What questions do you ask yourself about when to make noise, when to raise a point, when to amplify others, how to dig deeper?

Prayer

Feeling-filled Jesus,

you believed that prayer was a courtyard
with open doors,
welcoming all.

And when the courtyard started charging
you started charging.

Charge us, Jesus of Nazareth,
to change; to change towards a citizenship
of inclusion, not of profit.

Empty the coffers of our toxic valuations of value.
Because you believed in the worth
of true community.
And were willing to die for it.
Amen.

Lent 4 – John 3.14–21

Pádraig Ó Tuama

Introduction

In this week's conversation between Jesus and Nicodemus, we hear the words of Jesus – confident, confronting and causing a certain kind of conflict – asking over and over again: do you believe? What do you believe? Do you follow? What do you follow?

This is not a shibboleth controlling access to a heaven. Instead this is an invitation – albeit a confronting one – to respond. What do you say *back*? Of all the words available to you in your vocabulary, what would you say to this person who is asking you, truly, what you think, what you believe, what you follow?

Preparation

As you prepare for this week's text, take a moment to deliberately set aside old demands from religious threat and to willingly and generously grant yourself permission to say exactly what you think in response to a Jesus who – whatever else we think of him – always granted himself that same permission.[1]

Comment

From baptism and temptation through to Transfiguration and turning the tables in the temple, the theological and literary project of the texts this Lent season has been to help us *see* Jesus. For all the pieties associated with Lent – giving up things, taking up things, giving alms – the ultimate goal is to remove impediments to *seeing*; seeing Jesus in particular and seeing him in circumstances all around.

This week's text is an excerpt from the dialogue between Jesus and Nicodemus. John's Gospel – the latest one to be written (possibly around 90 CE, possibly later) – contains various extended dialogues; places the most elevated Christology alongside the most emotional depictions of Jesus; narrates only seven signs; has no mention of demons or the kingdom; and records the longest dinner speech in the New Testament.

It also features some binary themes: follow/don't follow; darkness/light; belief/unbelief; life/death. In this dialogue, some of these themes are seen: 'whoever believes in him may have eternal life'; 'whoever believes in him may not perish but may have eternal life'; 'those who believe in him are not condemned, but those who do not believe ... because they have not believed'; 'light has come into the world'; 'people loved darkness rather than the light'; 'all who do evil hate the light'; 'those who do what is true come to the light'. The confidence of voice given to the character of Jesus in this gospel account is, for me, confronting. It's a 'my way or the highway' voice.

This would have inevitably caused conflict among those who were observing him. It causes conflict, too, in those of us reading the text during Lent in this year of our Lord 2021, a year of pandemic, an era of populism, a time of untruth, fake news, vaccine conflicts, inequality, racism and distraction. What does it mean to look to this character of Jesus, whose self-assuredness is so clearly articulated?

Does the attention to these words and beliefs of Jesus of Nazareth in this week's gospel text console you, confuse you, challenge you or critique you? Or something else? What do you think of a character who, in a time of occupation by a foreign army, was able to hold attention on himself and use this attention to critique his co-religionists? What would you say back to someone who says, 'Those who believe in him are not condemned; but those who do not believe are condemned already'? Would you agree with him or argue with him?

Such binaries are, in my own opinion, a literary *function* rather than *fundamental* to this depiction of Jesus. He seemed to be interested in causing conflict in people who were attracted to him. He wanted them to speak their minds and was content to be an irritant in their lives until they spoke the truth to him. What are the conflicts that binary religious language cause in you? And – rather than deciding whether to accept it or reject it all outright – what do you say back? What is your self-understanding in conversation with the text? What is your argument back?

This is, I think, the invitation of the text. Not to think about whether you're condemned or not, but rather to think of what you'd actually say back to someone who was pushing and pushing and pushing. Pushing people to speak truthfully back to him, rather than to perform what they think will win them friends and influence. Jesus seemed uninterested in pandering to popularity – he regularly made life difficult for his friends and would-be followers.

What's helpful to remember is that in this fourth Gospel, sitting alongside such binary language from Jesus, is the most elevated theology of friendship we find in the Christian scriptures. Jesus, in this gospel, is not interested in telling his friends to love their enemies. He's interested in loving his friends till the end. This last supper depiction has him disrobe and wash the feet of those he loves. And even in this text, famous for being used as a battering ram about perishing and condemnation, the motivation of God towards the world is *love*, not despair. For God so *loved the world*. This is a demonstration of an incarnation that is interested in the argument of being alive, not the ambivalence of affectation.

So again. You. What do you say back? What do you assert? What could you say that would make Jesus look at you and see a friend who is willing to speak truthfully to him, as he speaks truthfully to you. Lent is not about chocolate or wine. Lent is about this. Look. Listen. Speak back. This is the word of the Lord speaking to you. This is you speaking back to the Word of the Lord.

Response

Once, when I was a school chaplain, one of the young people at a session asked me, *What do you think about Jesus?*

This was not a test or an opportunity to bear witness. This was an experience where a 12-year-old asked a serious question and wanted me to demonstrate truth and respect in the way I answered.

Growing up I had heard people preach fear-based sermons on 'when you reject me before people, I will reject you before God'. There were anxieties about evangelization that had been baked into my bones. But here, in a chaplaincy, with a kind and good and intelligent and curious 12-year-old, I was faced with a much more demanding – and, truthfully, a much more interesting – question. This young person wasn't asking to be converted or to be witnessed to. He was asking about my experience. He was asking me to tell a story from the literature of my own life.

I loved what he asked. After I offered him my answer, I asked him. How about you? What do you think? He spoke. I listened. I have never forgotten him. What about you? What do you think about Jesus?

Prayer

Strange man of Nazareth,

you poked and prodded people around you.
People who had power were provoked into questions,
people with curiosity, too; you scraped surfaces,
willing to risk irritation or aggression in the name
of truthful encounters.

In our lives – tired and under demand as they are in
this time of pandemic – enliven us by the kind of
conversation that is unforgettable. Meet us
with ourselves as you meet us.

Because this is the water of life. You
drank from it. You needed it.
So do we.
Amen.

Note

1 Another reflection on parts of this passage can be found at Lent
2A (p. 110).

Lent 5 – John 12.20–33

Pádraig Ó Tuama

Introduction

At times in faith communities, there can be a great unity: in prayer; with others; with self. At other times, we know, there can be a great chasm, a distance, a presence of absence. Sometimes the unity comes during a time of great peace, other times it can be felt even in the midst of tribulation. The same with the presence of absence: sometimes it is there in times of great peace; other times in great trial.

The gospel writers each depict Jesus' response to the circumstances leading up to his arrest, trial, torture and execution differently. Mark makes the presence of absence known: his Jesus ventures into the abyss where God is not. John, however, has a different approach to this. In the Jesus of John, we hear a voice consoled by the sense of unity he feels with God, even though he faces into an abyss.

There is no one way. I find strange consolation that the gospel writers depict this experience of unity or absence in different ways. Perhaps we are hearing more about the artists behind these gospel texts than we are perceiving the actual experience of Jesus as he goes through these awful trials. Whether you are in a time of plenty in your spirituality, or in the midst of a time of lack, you are in company, especially if you feel alone. As long as there have been gospels – and longer! – there has been the joint experience of the presence and the presence of the absence.[1]

Preparation

As you come to this week's text, take a moment to consider how, today, you are experiencing questions of presence in the practice of your prayer.

Comment

This text comes at a pivotal point in the Gospel of John. That gospel can be divided into two main parts: 'The Book of Signs' (John 1.19 to the end of chapter 12) and 'The Book of Glory' (chapter 13 to the end). The first narrates the seven signs that Jesus did in his public ministry. John's narration of these is longer, more characterful and more detailed than the other gospels' depictions. The culminating sign is the raising of Lazarus, after which the plot to kill Jesus takes particular administrative detail.

'The hour' is a motif throughout the Book of Signs, either as something to which Jesus speaks (e.g., 2.4; 4.2; 5.25) or as the reason why plots against him fail – 'his hour had not yet come' (7.30; 8.20). And now, in this lectionary text for this week, in response to hearing that some Greeks (symbolizing, perhaps, citizens of the wide world) wish to see him, Jesus says: 'The hour has come for the Son of Man to be glorified.'

In John's schema, the hour is the time when the Son of Man is glorified: by laying down his life for his friends; by going willingly to a place to which others would seek to force him; by showing a practice of service at the feet of his friends while others would seek to mock him by elevating him naked, tortured and exposed on the cross. As I think of it, the glory is less the torture device and more the poise of Jesus to show love, even to the end.

John's telling of this awful saga is one where he portrays a deep picture of Jesus' sense of unity with God. Jesus is aware of what is coming and a voice comes from heaven. He is troubled, yes, but he does not wish to be saved from the hour. He has glory promised him and the glory sounds like words of consolation, or thunder, or words for other people. Jesus' mission is being elevated, even to driving out the ruler of the world, and being lifted up – eventually – as a sign to draw all people to himself.

This way of telling the story puts a high Christology into the mouth of Jesus: he is aware of being loved; he is troubled but not undone; he has assurance of the way forward; and he sees glory on the other side of despair. There are times in our lives, when, in the face of difficulties, we have a deep assuredness and this assuredness keeps us steady.

Were we reading the Passion according to Mark, we would hear a different cry: a cry of abandonment, of forsakenness, a lament, an accusation even – Jesus choosing a line from a psalm used as a night prayer and erasing everything in it except the mournful accusation: 'My God, my God, why have you forsaken me?' The Jesus in John will say, 'Woman, here is your son', 'I am thirsty' and 'It is finished' from the cross, focused on a mission to the end: to provide for his mother, to drink the last cup of the Passover (which had been omitted from John's account of the meal) and to state that what he had come to accomplish had been accomplished.

There is no right way to narrate this. What I admire is that the gospel tradition narrates both the presence of the absence and the presence of the presence. We can find so many of our own personal experiences in the space between the tellings of Mark and John. At times in our spiritual life, we feel alone, but are not afraid; at other times we are surrounded, but are still undone. There is no conflict between these. We move back and forth, sometimes in the presence of consolation, other times in the presence of absence. Both are, it is important to say, important to notice, to see, to describe, to be in, to narrate, to reach out from, to reach out towards.

Response

As you think of your last year, what have been your experiences of the presence of the presence and the absence of the presence? When have they oscillated?

Ignatius of Loyola urged his followers to do a review of their prayer at the end of every prayer time they had. When I was going through the spiritual exercises, I landed on meteorological metaphors for this practice. Had the prayer been like an overcast day? Or was it a soft twilight? Was I standing at a crashing shore, or trying to swim away from a whirlpool? Was I watching something unfold in the dawn? Or was I wishing it could stay one way and not change?

Whatever language or metaphor you use to describe this, it's a useful exercise and especially useful to make a small note of it – a line or two, nothing demanding – and then to review this at the end of a week, a month, a season. Noticing how the experience of presence and absence moves throughout your week can give you a sense of wise detachment the next time you feel absent: absent from yourself, your loved ones, your prayer.

Prayer

Mysterious Jesus

what we do not know
is what all this was like for you.
Your friends told stories
and their friends wrote them down.
And we wonder:
were you in the presence of great presence?
Or were you in the presence
of an absence?

In all our experiences of presence
and absence,
help us remember the story to which we are called.

A story of love, of generosity,
of justice, of truth.

Knowing that presence will come and go,
but the call to love
never fails.
Amen.

Note

1 See Holy Week Tuesday for alternative reflections on this text
(p. 204).

Lent 6 Liturgy of the Palms – Mark 11.1–11

Pádraig Ó Tuama

Introduction

We are in a particular geography for Palm Sunday. We hear of Jesus approaching Jerusalem, passing through Bethphage and Bethany, as well as the Mount of Olives and the temple. These names are so associated with Passiontide events in our minds that it can sometimes be difficult to see these as villages and towns with their own stories: scandals, markets, griefs, births, changes, festivals, delights, marriages, family feuds.

This year, Palm Sunday comes into a world that is busy with so much else. So many of us are coping with the awful complexities of Covid. And, on top of that, many are dealing with the ongoing trauma of systemic oppression: racism, misogyny, ageism, etc.

What can come among the difficulties of our lives that might cause us to stop, and look, and say 'Hosanna', say 'Blessed'? In difficult lives, it can be difficult to know where to look for hope. As we enter into this Palm Sunday, we invite you to take a little time to consider what it is that holds your gaze in troubled times.

Comment

The Gospel of Mark is famous for its depiction of Jesus' reticence – 'The Messianic Secret'. Explanations abound: Jesus wished his status to be revealed in works, not words; Jesus wished to be able to move about safely; Jesus is portrayed as a type of Odysseus, a figure from Greek mythology who also disguised his identity ... each explanation has a lot of richness to it.

Whatever the explanation about Jesus' secrecy for much of the Marcan narration, his arrival into Jerusalem is a marked end to this secrecy. Whereas up until now it is demons that proclaim, 'I know who you are! The Christ of God' (and even they were silenced), it is now the population of Jerusalem who shout and praise and wave palms, laying their cloaks on the road as Jesus enters the city on a colt. This is an inauguration from the people by the people. This entrance is not orchestrated with pomp and ceremony, it is not choreographed via threats from someone on the other end of the symbology; rather, it is one that emerges organically. Jesus' reputation – despite all of his secrecies – has spread like wildfire. The people are looking to him, more than likely looking for some kind of deliverance from the Roman Empire, the ruler of which could only dream about a rapturous, spontaneous welcome such as this.

Jesus' certitude and authority are shown clearly too. He tells his disciples where to procure a colt – one that has never been ridden – and gives them an explanation that is as vague as it is assertive (v.3). Whatever the personal stories of mystification among the owners of the animal – or the animal itself – what we are seeing here is a sense of embodied authority. Authority is a thread throughout Mark – the destructive lust for it by empire and the intuitive embodiment of it by Jesus. (For a study of the theme of authority in Mark, read through 1.22, 27; 2.10; 3.15; 6.7; 11.28, 29, 33.)

Much conflict can gather around the question of authority: people might say, 'Who do they think they are, telling me what to do?' or, 'I wish they'd just do their job and manage' or, 'They are listening to the wrong people' or, 'The way they act at work, it's criminal'. The experience of being on the receiving end of an authority that you deem too authoritative, presumptive or ineffective can get deep into the psyche.

Another side of the equation is also true: it can be a crisis to be seen to have authority. Many people in religious leadership may feel as if people look at them as though they have authority but they might say they have title but no *actual* authority. It can be a crisis to be in power, as much as it can be a crisis to detect it. Some people abdicate the authority they have. Others assume authority they don't have. The world unfolds. It is evening, it is morning, the next day.

The Jesus of Mark – and, it must be said, the Jesus of the six weeks of our Lenten series – has been one who has gone back and forth in terms of his public and private life. He seeks to be in control, directed neither by empire nor ego, populism nor popularity. He – and, it seems, he alone – understands the lonely sacrifices he will face. And he keeps his eye on those, using authority not as a means to its own end, but as a way of moving on towards what he sees is his call, his voice, his vocation. Authority is a tool, not a goal, in this gospel. It is a sign, a sign pointing towards something not itself. For Jesus, it is a pathway towards liberation, although even that is misunderstood: many, for very understandable reasons, saw liberation from empire as the goal, whereas Jesus saw a more complex liberation, one that would deepen his loneliness and his call.

Response

What are the authority-related conflicts you're living with these days? Some of those will be small, some of those will be large.

What is at the heart of the question of authority for you in these conflicts? Is it that someone is abusing authority? Or not using it at all? Is it that someone has an idea of what you should be doing with the authority they think you have? Is it something entirely different?

In all of these conflicts, it is wise to pay attention to the conflict about the conflict, too.

What are ways you can share the burden of this? Perhaps it is only by telling the story; this may seem small, but it may still help a little.

Prayer

Jesus,
person of privacy and publicity,
popular – for a while – but not populist;
you held your centre,
based on what you understood to be your call.

Help us to hear a call,
not to greatness or grandiosity,
not to position or prominence
but to the deepest call of all:
love, creativity and justice.

May this carry us, through
the lauds and lamentations
of our lives.

And may we be faithful to love, creativity
and justice, as you were.
Amen.

Lent Year C

Ash Wednesday – Matthew 6.1–6, 16–21

Janet Foggie

Introduction

On Ash Wednesday, we think of our own responsibilities. Conflicts within church may often stem from judgements made that brand the 'other' as hypocritical. Texts such as this lend themselves to misuse, especially within a conflict situation. Today, we are considering what practices we may follow that are like the prayer on the street corner: more for show than for love itself. Perhaps in our generation, we may find it easier to brag, blog or tweet about our beliefs than to serve, love and cherish others.

'For where your treasure is, there your heart will be also.' Jesus' closing words are a good starting point for reading this passage. It is too easy to simply read the passage one way, pointing a finger at the hypocrites, and not reading it as a challenge to our own piety. If, before starting, we ground ourselves with the idea of our personal unique treasure, and why we value it, then we might find the passage easier to hear.

Preparation

- What is your treasure?
- What would you say were the most important things in your life?
- What is the true purpose of religious faith or practice?
- What is the most precious thing about your faith for you?
- Do your 'treasure' and your 'faith' bring about a conflict in your heart?

Comment

The conflicts in this text leap off the page at us. There is no need for deep reading or careful analysis to see conflict in almost every line – and it is a conflict started by Jesus. He sets up two groups of people, the audience and the 'hypocrites'. The charge of hypocrisy, of saying one thing and doing another, is one of the strongest reprimands Jesus uses – as the language he uses in Matthew 23 when preaching against it makes clear: 'For you are like whitewashed tombs, which on the outside look beautiful, but inside they are full of the bones of the dead and of all kinds of filth.'

In this passage, the hypocrites are accused of using religious ritual as a means of garnering and receiving praise from others. In contrast the audience are instructed not to be like these people – for whom receiving that praise in the moment is their reward – but instead to pray to God in secret and God who sees in secret will reward them in due course.

The assumption that the hypocrites will always be 'other people' is the danger here – not just for the disciples, followers or eavesdroppers of Jesus' original audience – but also for readers now. We are reminded throughout the passage that human actions are what are being judged here. In the story of the sheep and the goats later in Matthew (25.31–46), Jesus describes two groups again: sheep, who have done what God wanted without necessarily knowing it, and goats, who have not done what God wanted. It is not the profession of faith, but the actions of kindness that Jesus judges.

Deciding that other groups whose ecclesiastical or theological ideas are not the same as your own are 'the hypocrites' is not an armchair sport devised by Jesus to keep us guessing. Seeking out people with whom we disagree, online or in person, just to tell them so, is not the solution Jesus sets out for us here. Instead we are called upon to act in accordance with God's command to love our neighbour and to do so in secret. The eternal judgement is God's alone, not ours with which to measure or weigh our fellow Christians.

Conflicts within church may often stem from judgements made that brand the 'other' as hypocritical. Texts such as this lend themselves to misuse, especially within a conflict situation. This is why it is important to come back for a second time to the idea of heavenly treasure. What is it that we treasure most? Why is that the dearest thing to us? What does it say about God that he gave us this treasure as a gift? How do we understand this treasure to be eternal?

Once we have identified our treasure, some conflicts may be solved by reordering our priorities. It may be that if we focus on what gives our spirits treasure, move our prayers and our good deeds into the private realm and refuse to try and expose the hypocrisy of others, the issue we felt was an unsolvable conflict will in fact slowly diminish for us.

Response

Sometimes we offer rewards for the return of lost property, or to help obtain information about a crime. At other times the reward which comes from a good ethical choice is more subtle, but is there nonetheless. Think about a time when you did a good deed, without meaning to be rewarded for it, but in some way or another you did receive an immediate positive experience. How does it feel to be rewarded? How does it feel to be helped without being able to offer a reward?

If you use social media platforms you might also like to consider the following questions.

In Jesus' day, news was shared mainly by word of mouth and the street corner was a hub of social interaction, gossip and news. In what ways would you see social media as the street corner of today? What would be your definition of a 'troll' or 'trolling' behaviour? How do we share news of the good things we have done – and are we rewarded by tweets, likes, shares and followers? Is your social media set up in such a way that you are kind to others and that your good deeds are done in secret?

Prayer

God of the secret –
who seeks out those who love in secret, who care in secret,
work for the poor and the outcast,
but not for praise or immediate reward –
enable me to be braver in my secret kindness,
respectful of others, gentle in my heart,
repenting of my hypocrisy and any harm it may have done.
God of the secret, hold my heart in secret,
that it may begin to dwell on earth
with the priorities of heaven.
Through Jesus Christ
who offered treasure that will not spoil or fade.
Amen.

Lent 1 – Luke 4.1–13

Janet Foggie

Introduction

Ethics is often seen as a dry discipline, a waste of time. But in many of our daily decisions, concerning food, power, risk taking and authority, ethics quickly come to the fore. In this story, making the right ethical decision is what allows Jesus to defeat the devil. It is possibly too easy to focus on the spiritual dimension of the passage and not look at the actual application it has to the temptations we face in our daily lives and how we deal with them. This text is very familiar for many and so it can be a challenge to see afresh the truths contained within it.

Read the text and think about what it tells us of Jesus' ethics.

Comment

The temptations of Jesus demonstrate and underline for us the very human moments when we have to face ethical decisions: when we, or perhaps our children, are hungry; when we are tempted by political power – in both the working world and the domestic setting, power tempts us as it tempted Jesus; and finally, in taking risks, there is a temptation in recklessness and in the too-firm belief in faith as a 'rescue service' or a 'safety net'.

When humans come to argue about ethics, there is often an early loss in the actual ethical behaviour of those engaged in that discussion. In the era of the Reformation, for example, Erasmus and Luther disagreed on the subject of whether humans have freedom of choice – a dispute which has run through the ages of Christian ethical thinking. During the Reformation, disputes like this led to torture, disfigurements and deaths on both sides. It seems ironic to us in the twenty-first century that a religion of love, following Jesus who refused all the temptations placed before him, might be induced into entertaining such antagonism and accepting its outcomes. Yet even today, there are Christians who feel it their duty to correct, oppose or even harm – psychologically if not physically – other Christians simply because of their ethical beliefs.

If we think for a moment about whether we ourselves believe or feel free to choose, this changes how we read this text. Is Jesus tempted as a human is tempted, because of his humanity? If so, then we are all free to choose to resist temptation. However, it may be that Jesus was only free to choose because he is divine, and that we are 'lesser mortals' for whom temptation and its consequences are predestined by an all-powerful God. So what does this choice, of whether to accept free will or not, change for us in how we read the text?

When we find ourselves in situations of conflict, it can be an easy first move to draw a metaphorical line somewhere in the definitions of ethical or unethical, free or unfree, truly-a-Christian or not-a-Christian. We feel the need to identify a group to which we belong, and therefore a group to which we do not belong. If this temptation had been curbed in the century of Luther and Erasmus, much pain might have been avoided both at the time and going forward.

So – is Jesus lied to by the devil, who tells him that he, the devil, has been given the authority to ascribe the leadership of the kingdoms of the world? Or in your estimation is there a devil who truly has this power? Either way, the definition of 'in-group' and 'out-group' people can only be part of the false kingdoms, the human-based groups of our world.

It seems to me the ruling of kingdoms, like the drawing of groups, is about factions and a negative model of power. Jesus cuts through with his answer, 'Worship the Lord your God, and serve only him.'

Response

Think about a situation in which you have power. It could be giving a talk, managing others at work, organizing the local volunteer group, holding a conversation, caring for people younger than yourself, even just cooking a meal or hosting guests. Then consider the following questions: how does it feel to hold power? How does it change your choices or your tone?

Who in your ordinary life has less power than you? Who do you most regularly interrupt? Or forget to listen to carefully? Who do you step in front of, literally or metaphorically? How does this passage speak to you about wielding power?

Alternatively, draw a diagram of the groups to which you belong – maybe some overlap, maybe not. Is there anywhere that you feel your group identity might conflict with Christ's solution to power-grabs of 'Worship the Lord your God, and serve only him'? Does this enable you to see conflict between groups differently? Or do you find you can read the temptations of Jesus and yet feel you have still been consistently right all along?

Prayer

God of the kingdoms of this world,
we seek to worship you and serve only you.
Enable us to understand the places
where we make judgements,
draw lines, make distinctions, impose definitions.
Let us see the factions of this world for what they are,
and free us to live in humility with our labels,
our groups and our kingdoms.
In and through our Lord Jesus Christ
who defied temptation by directing himself back to you,
Amen.

Lent 2 – Luke 13.31–35

Janet Foggie

Introduction

In our reading today, Jesus receives a death threat. I wonder what the tone, the level of hostility and animosity was as the Pharisees came to Jesus and told him, 'Get away from here, for Herod wants to kill you.' Were they trying to help Jesus by bringing a warning? Or were they threatening him?

While you read the passage, think about the serious nature of a death threat and the effect it has on mental health and well-being. Why does Jesus respond as he does? Is his response what you would expect?

Comment

Jesus did not live in a world of social media and easy mass communication. The Pharisees had to physically visit him to pass on the news of Herod's intention to kill him. Reading the passage with this news as a death threat, and not a kindly warning, Jesus' response of 'Go and tell that fox' suggests that he heard the warning as a threat and was aware (especially given the fate of his cousin John the Baptist) that Herod meant to carry it out.

In the United Kingdom, and in many other jurisdictions, a threat of serious harm, including death, is a criminal offence and carries a serious consequence if a conviction is brought. For Jesus, the threatening power had the confidence of the Roman administration behind it. This threat was being made by Herod Antipas, who was tetrarch, or joint ruler, of Galilee and Perea. Antipas was a client-ruler. Although as such he was not technically styled a king, the use of this term in Scripture suggests that ordinary people commonly thought of him in that role.

In contrast, Jesus, as a vulnerable, homeless, religious teacher, would have no recourse to justice. He places this threat upon his own life in the context of other prophets and missionaries who had been stoned in the city of Jerusalem.

In our age of social media, death threats, harassment online and by text, and other forms of abuse have become serious issues. Celebrities and public figures are frequently the target of negative social media attention. Members of Parliament in the UK, such as Mhairi Black, Anas Sawar, Anne-Marie Trevelyan and others have all had abusive or threatening tweets directed at them. The murder of Labour MP Jo Cox in 2016, in a politically motivated crime, demonstrates that while the sheer volume of online abuse means that it cannot all be intended to be put into action, the reality is that there is nevertheless always a risk of the ultimate cost being paid by public figures from those with extremist views.

If this is the case for public figures, it is also true for private citizens, and, unfortunately, those in minority sections of our community, such as LGBTQI, racial, cultural and religious minorities, suffer a disproportionate amount of online abuse or harassment.

Jesus does acknowledge the risk that he may be killed and suggests this will not occur outside Jerusalem. It may seem odd, given his rebuttal of the death threat in which he says he will simply continue to heal the sick and cast out demons, that he then expresses sympathy for Jerusalem, the seat of the ruler who is threatening to kill him. It would be more than could be expected, surely, for a victim of abuse to have any sympathy with those who were threatening them with death. Yet it would be hard to argue, given that Jesus has just said that it would be 'impossible for a prophet to be killed outside of Jerusalem', that he doesn't include in his next statement those who wish to kill him:

'Jerusalem, Jerusalem, the city that kills the prophets and stones those who are sent to it! How often have I desired to gather your children together as a hen gathers her brood under her wings, and you were not willing!'

In this text, Jesus identifies with a mother hen. He describes the natural behaviour of a hen when threatened with danger, to gather her chicks under her wings. Yet, he exclaims that the people of Jerusalem are not willing to come into his comforting, mothering wingspan. Instead, they reject him, and for now he will leave to continue his teaching, healing and ministering elsewhere a while longer.

Response

- Think about the ways in which social media enables people to threaten others anonymously or from a distance. What part does allowing anonymity online play in exacerbating abusive or threatening speech?
- Why do distinctive characteristics, for example being a turban-wearing Sikh, a hijab-wearing Muslim, an 'out' trans person, or having an obvious physical or social disability, lead to a person suffering more of this kind of abusive language online?
- How would we extend Jesus' mothering, sheltering wing in situations of abuse or hate-crime? Would we consider only the victims to be worthy of shelter, or like Jesus can we extend shelter to all of Jerusalem? Under Jesus' sheltering wing, how do we work with victims with dignity and solidarity to end stigma and discrimination?
- Those whom Jesus most wanted to shelter under his mothering wing refused the invitation. How do we, as a society, cope with those who refuse to accept goodness as a method of dealing with others, or as a way of challenging behaviour which is hostile?

Prayer

Today we pray with a consciousness that Jesus was not able to prevent the brutal end to his own journey. We know that those who plotted and threatened to kill him prevailed. Enable us, as we try to understand the brutality and injustice of hate crimes, to understand the journey Jesus walked.

Lenten God,
it may be too much for us
to grasp the mother-hen love of Jesus.
That one so frail, vulnerable and poor,
facing threats to his own life,
could extend a warm, secure, loving wing
to those who threatened him.

Comfort us, under that same shelter,
Lenten God,
open our eyes to see, understand and protest
the trauma for those who live with threats,
always unwarranted,
unfair, unjustified and unacceptable.

Lenten God,
we step forward with humble feet,
in the hope that we may make a gentle word carry far,
firmly resolved to speak into abuse and harassment
with calm, honest resolution.
Through our Lord Jesus Christ,
Amen.

Lent 3 – Luke 13.1–9

Janet Foggie

Introduction

The theme of this Sunday's text is repentance. Although most Bibles make a paragraph shift in the middle of the text, between verses five and six, it is useful to read the text as a single paragraph and to think of the common theme of repentance in both halves. As you read, try to connect the story of the fig tree with the other examples given by Jesus. Scholars can't agree on what the incidents involving the falling tower of Siloam and the Galileans killed by Pilate actually were, but we don't need to know everything Jesus' audience knew to get an understanding of the contrast between those who died violently or by accident and the salvation of the life of an unfruitful tree by a gardener.

Preparation

What is the relationship between repentance and life for Jesus' audience? Can we imagine them all tied up with gossip about recent violent deaths only to hear Jesus challenge all their assumptions?

In what way does the story of the gardener and the fig tree speak of repentance and life?

Comment

The popular song by Billy Joel, 'Only the Good Die Young', might sum up a general social attitude today that the loss of a young life is tragic and mourned deeply. All the best points of a person who dies young are emphasized as we try to come to terms with an occurrence that is, in some societies at least, relatively rare. For the people of Jesus' time, the death of the young – babies, children and young adults – was a very common happening and a somewhat different social view was held. They believed that those who died young, especially in violent or traumatic circumstances, must have done something bad to deserve it.

We can read in the book of Job a story about the theology of suffering and see scriptures there that challenge this widely held view. However, even though that book was in the scriptures Jesus' contemporaries read and knew, there were still many who believed that an early death was the result of sin.

Second, it is important to think about the word 'perish' (from *apollymi* in the Greek). This is a word that can also mean 'lost' (as in Matthew 10.6 – the lost sheep) or 'destroy' (as in Matthew 12.14 – when the Pharisees planned to destroy Jesus). Jesus tells his audience that if they believe the Galileans and the people killed by the tower of Siloam were especially wicked because of their fate, then the audience will be lost in the same way. He seems to be saying that the belief that premature death is a consequence of wickedness is one which can prevent true repentance and thus cause destruction or loss.

But this is only part of the story. Cutting people off before they have time to repent and change is an equally negative action. The fig tree in the following part of the passage represents the person who is yet to find the fruitful blessing of repenting from their sins. That fundamental human action of feeling sorry for the wrongs we have done and intending to put them right is analogous to a tree which does not fruit being weeded and fed manure.

The organic gardener, Charles Dowding, has spent his lifetime pioneering the skills of no-dig gardening. He has proved that better yields are gained, not when we dig soil, but when we *feed* it. Jesus similarly provides a model of fruit husbandry that feeds the poorly performing tree. Once fed and cared for, the tree may well fruit the following year and therefore be saved.

Loss and death are tied together in the Greek verb which Jesus here uses to mean 'to perish'. On the opposite side, in feeding the soil, and tending the ground, life and salvation are balanced.

What would be the equivalent of weeding and manuring (feeding) a human relationship so that repentance and a resultant forgiveness might flourish?

Response

If you have access to a garden, set aside a piece of ground to try no-dig gardening (there's a reference to one of Charles Dowding's books in the notes below to help you and you can also find information on his website).[1] You will need some cardboard, a good lot of compost and some seeds. Instead of digging over the ground, just put the cardboard down on top of the ground (weeds, grass and all) in a good thick layer, then add a good thick layer of the compost. You can plant your seeds directly into this compost – late March is the ideal time of year to try this with carrots, peas or beans. Then in summer, you can enjoy the life-giving reward of having the garden that you fed, in turn, feed you.

OR

Is there a relationship in your life that has withered or is lost? What spiritual feeding would be needed to make that relationship grow and flourish again? What weeds might need to be pulled? Can you think of it as a fig tree that has not fruited yet instead of an opportunity lost? Figs hold their fruit for two years – they develop in the first year, and ripen in the second. Do you have the patience for a two- or three-year redemptive process in that relationship?

Prayer

Generous God, if we think of fasting, denying and giving
  things up for Lent,
remind us instead of your bountiful harvest
that feeds the barren, finds the lost and saves those who
  may perish.
Turn our hearts around to understand the no-dig forgiveness
  you preached.
May we, for our part, not dig and probe at our hurts,
but instead openly repent and generously forgive others
in order to see new fruit form in our relationships.
In the love of the good gardener who saved the fig tree,
Amen.

Note

1 Charles Dowding, *Organic Gardening: The Natural No-dig Way*
(Cambridge: Green Books, 2013). See also www.charlesdowding.co.uk.

Lent 4 – Luke 15.1–3, 11b–32

Trevor Williams

Introduction

The conclusion of the first section of last week's gospel (Luke 13.1–9) saw Jesus saying to those listening: 'Unless you repent you will likewise perish.' If this was the final word, it would give the impression that God's focus is judgement and punishment. This week's gospel is one of the best-known passages in the Bible – the story of the prodigal son. It's a story that we love – but it is a story of two halves. There are two sons and the elder, the prodigal's brother, deserves much closer attention than we sometimes feel inclined to give him.

Preparation

What is your response to the word 'repent'? Is it a positive response or a largely negative one? Can you analyse why?

Have you thought about the fact that repentance could really be an invitation to find a new direction towards abundant life, avoiding the calamitous consequences of the direction in which you were heading? Does that understanding change any of your responses?

These are themes that can be found within the familiar words of this wonderful story.

Comment

As thoroughly modern beings, we like to think of ourselves as autonomous individuals who decide what we want, when we want it and how to get it. However, René Girard, theologian and philosopher of social science, has made us aware that this is an illusion. The reality is that we live in relationship with those around us – and our desires, attitudes and behaviours are heavily influenced by those relationships. Hence, rather than autonomy, we are constantly influenced by 'the Other' and measure ourselves against them. We are drawn to those who appear to have more than we do and feel we deserve to have the same as them. Rivalry can drive us to seek the upper hand, to be better than they are and to posses over and above what these Others hold. But there is a dark side here, and such rivalry can lead, ultimately, to violence.

The prodigal son lives and works on the family farm with his father and elder brother. But in his mind he becomes convinced that there must be more, that he is somehow missing out – that this secure home life on his father's farm is in fact a prison, preventing him from fulfilling his dreams. He is in rivalry not with an actual Other but with an imagined 'good life'. In the vividly told story, he lives the dream for a while but then reality strikes and the dream becomes a nightmare.

And then, Jesus tells his hearers, he 'came to himself'. He decides to return home, realizing that, as he has squandered his place in the family with its privileges and inheritance, all he can do is to plead with his father for a position as a 'hired hand'. But then the story takes its unexpected turn.

Every day the father was on the look out for his lost son. And one day, there he was, in the distance, returning home! The father runs, put his arms around him and kisses him, putting on a special party to celebrate the return of his beloved son. He is extravagantly reinstated as a full member of the family.

Observing this lavish attention given to his brother, the elder son feels ignored. His father pleads with him to join the party – but the elder son can't stand it and excludes himself from the celebration. He feels, by comparison with this prodigal, that he is the slave, a non-person, neglected, taken for granted, the lowest of the low. He is in an emotional pig sty. Here is rivalry, with violence of attitude, if not action.

These stories prompt us in many different situations to consider what we 'hope to gain' and what we 'fear to lose'. The prodigal was led astray by what he hoped to gain. The elder son was consumed with jealousy because of what he feared he had lost. Both were fantasies fuelled by rivalry of 'the Other'. In contrast to these destructive fantasies, it is the loving action of the father that enables new life and new possibilities. The loving of our neighbour – the desiring for the other that which we wish for ourselves and then making this possible – stands in stark contrast to the dark road that rivalry opens up in front of us.

Repentance is that change of mind, that deciding to follow a new direction, that holds open the possibility of new beginnings for us all.

Response

Each son's experience interrogates our attitudes and values as individuals and as a society: the prodigal's quest suggests a parallel with the aspiration of our consumerist culture; and the elder son's jealousy of his brother seems to blind him to all that is good and all he could enjoy in his situation. They can also shine a light on our experiences of conflict, helping us examine whether a gain/loss scenario with its associated hopes, fears, and rivalries is part of the dynamic we need to work to change, or to help others to change.

Prayer

God beyond rivalry,
our desire to have more,
to be more
to achieve more
than others
can lead us badly astray.

In Christ you walked among us
showing a different way,
a way not dominated and directed by rivalry.

May the way of the father guide us,
to support the weak,
to encourage the fearful,
to welcome the estranged.
In the name of he
who is the way, the truth and the life.
Amen.

Lent 5 – John 12.1–8

Trevor Williams

Introduction

Let's take a moment to think about gifts:

- What is the most memorable gift you have received?
- Why does it stick out in your memory?
- In giving a gift to someone you love, what is it you hope to convey?
- What makes a gift appropriate?
- What makes a gift inappropriate?

John is different from the synoptic gospels: it has a high proportion of original material, the stories that have synoptic parallels often contain more detail and they are presented quite differently. He frequently uses the contrast of opposites in a highly literary style, loves symbols and signs and appealing to the imagination and empathy of his audience.

Today's reading is a good example. Mark (14.3–9) and Matthew (26.6–13) both tell of a woman who anoints Jesus' head with costly perfume, that the disciples protest at the 'waste' and that Jesus rebukes them, saying that this is a preparation of his body for burial. Luke (7.36–50) has a sinful woman anointing Jesus' feet, Jesus contrasting her generosity with the lack of this shown by Simon, his host, and publicly forgiving her sin. John's version is different again in significant ways – so why has he given us this story in this way?[1]

Comment

At the heart of our reading is an act of anointing – an expression of the most extraordinary generosity. But before considering this, it is worth noting the way John tells the story – and as is typical of him, it is laced with multiple suggestions that fill out the symbolic interpretation. First, it is 'six days before the Passover'. The writer makes it impossible for us not to see that this event foreshadows the cross, and the anointing as a preparation for death. The anointing also expresses John's view of the cross as portraying both Jesus' death and exaltation. Anointing is part of the consecration of a king or priest, so by this anointing Jesus is declared king and priest; and this kingship is repeatedly referred to in John's account of the trial. Anointing is also used in healing and, as Lazarus was present at the meal, we are reminded that he was brought back to life by Jesus, which in turn prefigures the resurrection of Jesus himself. This is all part of the rich symbolic backdrop to the tapestry whose central subject is Mary's gift to Jesus.

Her extraordinary generosity is in the context of hospitality and a shared meal between Jesus, his disciples and a family with whom they have a close relationship. Lazarus is present as a focus for gratitude to Jesus; Martha serves the meal she has prepared, her particular act of gratitude. But it is Mary's extravagance in using such costly perfume (it would have cost almost a year's salary for a manual worker) to anoint Jesus' feet that holds our attention ... and that so offends Judas.

Here we have a highly charged conflict. Mary's costly generosity is targeted as being a waste, but more, as being morally wrong since it squandered the opportunity of doing good for many needy people. Does Judas not have a point? Should we take his side in this conflict? And how do we understand Jesus' response to Judas, which, from the Greek, literally means, 'Leave her alone so that she may keep it [the perfume] for the day of my burial'? To me it seems that this perfume may have been acquired for the body of Lazarus at the time of his death and is now given to Jesus as an act of profound gratitude. It is worth noting that the response of Jesus to Judas is gentle considering the heat of the moment! 'Leave her alone ...' – 'Come off it, Judas!' perhaps. But whereas Jesus intervenes to calm the tension, the writer of John's Gospel actively sides against Judas – designating him a thief and a pilferer of the common purse.

But how can we understand Jesus' subsequent comment about the poor? He was probably referring to a passage in Deuteronomy 15 that condemns a grudging attitude towards those in need and proposes an alternative liberal and perpetual generosity. Jesus is not excusing anyone the care of those in need, this should be our way of life!

The core of Judas' dispute with Mary is about the deployment of resources – which he regards her as needlessly wasting. So what value did her act have? First, her action was prompted by gratitude and faith. I imagine it was just something that she felt she should do. It wasn't so much thought out but, knowing Jesus as she did, it felt right. It wasn't a matter of belief or head knowledge – she can't have known what was to happen to Jesus within a week – it was a matter of the heart. In the light of Jesus' death, her act symbolizes central themes in John, that of Jesus' kingship through his death and exaltation. As with so many others who placed their trust in Jesus and were commended for their faith, Mary is commended for what she did.

From John's perspective, Mary's anointing, the wiping of Jesus' feet with her hair, prefigures the last act of Jesus with his disciples when he washes their feet. Is it even possible that Jesus got the idea for this gesture symbolizing generous service from this moment, adapting what Mary had done when she anointed his feet with perfume? If this is so, then Mary's act of extravagant generosity was also instrumental in forming the template of how the disciples of Jesus should love others.

While that may be speculation, what we do know is that an act of generosity has the potential of 'seeding' further acts of generous service. Here I believe we touch the heart of today's reading. Do you agree?

Response

The story offers us a number of pointers for reflecting on conflict.

Judas prejudges Mary's action, without fully understanding her motivation or the significance of the act. Can you think of a time when you have fallen into that trap of jumping to incorrect conclusions in judging other people? What was the outcome? How might we avoid falling into this particular temptation?

An assumption that lies behind this story is that Jesus accepted the presence of Judas as one of his close group of disciples. Judas is adjudged (by John at least) as a thief – if Jesus knew of this, why did he continue to associate with Judas? Or was it enough for Jesus that Judas, flawed as he was, wanted to be a disciple and thus his imperfections were not a bar to him being part of the inner group trusted with the work of the kingdom? How do, or should, we respond in situations in which we are involved where we do not quite trust the motives or integrity of one of the other players? Does generosity have a role here, and if so, how?

There is overt conflict here about the deployment of resources. Are you aware of parallels to this today around how we personally or collectively as a church (or other group) allocate resources? How can we approach such situations constructively?

Prayer

Open-hearted God,
Jesus created an inclusive community of disciples,
each with gifts and faults, strengths and weaknesses.
We give you thanks that your generous inclusion
is extended also to us – flawed as we too are.
May we be transformed by your loving acceptance
that like Mary, we may be extravagantly generous
in the service of others.
Amen.

Note

1 Other reflections on this text can be found in the Holy Week section (pp. 201, 229).

Lent 6 Liturgy of the Palms – Luke 19.28–40

Trevor Williams

Introduction

Jerusalem plays an important role in Luke's narrative: Jesus 'set his face to Jerusalem' early on (Luke 9.51–53) and thereafter Luke repeatedly underlines that Jesus is on his way to the city (13.22, 33–34; 17.11; 18.31; 19.11). Luke's Gospel is, at its heart, Jesus' journey to Jerusalem: he begins and ends the story there (2.22–30; 24.52–53) and he notes that Jesus and his family return to Jerusalem every Passover (4.41–50).

This final entry into Jerusalem in today's passage brings Luke's life of Jesus close to its climax. The timing of this final visit is important – Passover was the feast when the story of the liberation of God's people from slavery was celebrated.

Preparation

For Jesus' disciples, the final entry of Jesus into Jerusalem was very special. A cause of great celebration!

- What is your most vivid experience of 'winning'?
- What were your feelings?
- How did you celebrate?
- Did you share the experience with others? Who?

Comment

We all love to chant when our side is winning. This was no different.

But too much enthusiasm isn't welcomed by any religious establishment – people power challenges elite leadership. So, the Pharisees ask Jesus to use his influence to bring some order and decency back to the scene. To give them the benefit of the doubt, they may not have been hostile to Jesus but merely giving him some common-sense advice, given the occasion. Under the Roman Empire, life was harsh – people were subjected to humiliation, the loss of freedom, crushing taxes, military rule and judicial execution. To celebrate Passover, with its story of liberation from slavery, was political dynamite, and every Passover the Roman authorities were on high alert. But despite the obvious risk, Jesus refuses their advice and refuses to silence the crowd of disciples, saying, 'If they keep quiet, these stones will start shouting.'

Jesus deliberately chooses Passover and its celebration as a vehicle to proclaim his message. This was always his priority over everything else. The scene recalls the prophecy in Zechariah 9.9 and the crowd respond accordingly. But if we read on a little in Zechariah's prophecy, we then fill out the meaning of the earlier words:

'I, the LORD, will take away war chariots and horses from Israel and Jerusalem. Bows that were made for battle will be broken. I will bring peace to nations, and your king will rule from sea to sea.' (Zechariah 9.10, CEV)

By riding on a colt, Jesus enacts the heart of Zechariah's message in declaring that the rule of God would bring peace from sea to sea.

There is agreement between Jesus and the crowd about the destination of the journey – peace. However, as becomes clear, there is no agreement on the way to get there. The crowd's understanding was a dangerous mixture of political fundamentalism and religious fervour. In proclaiming Jesus as king, they were praising the one who would, they believed, gain victory over the Romans. This was a celebration about winning. This was the excitement of gaining freedom from their oppressors. So the crowd were shouting, for Home Rule! Stop the Killings! Cut the Taxes! Say NO to Caesar! Soldiers go home! Free the People! ... and eventually Free Barabbas!

As someone once said, when the God you worship has the same enemies as you, you know you are worshipping an idol. Palm Sunday is part of Holy Week. The road to Jerusalem was the road to the cross. This was Jesus' message of peace – one that redefines power, showing that it can be creative not destructive, liberating not oppressive, freeing not limiting. The power of Jesus is not the power of the despot, or the power of politics. It is not the power of someone *over* others, it is the power of love *for* others. Jesus travels towards the cross, knowing that love challenges political interests. Love is not about winners over losers, it is winning *for all*.

In the violent context of military rule and paramilitary resistance, Jerusalem is inevitably a powder keg. As the expectations of the crowd escalate, with their hopes of ousting the Romans, Jesus' commitment to non-violence – which they can neither understand nor accept – effectively lights the touch paper. And when he resists their violent intentions against the Romans, refusing to offer any defence other than that he is the king they had rightly proclaimed, the violence within spills out and needs a target: the cross was the inevitable consequence when Jesus chose the power of love over the love of power:

> Let each of you look not to your own interests, but to the interests of others. Let the same mind be in you that was in Christ Jesus, who, though he was in the form of God, did not regard equality with God as something to be exploited, but emptied himself, taking the form of a slave, being born in human likeness. And being found in human form, he humbled himself and became obedient to the point of death – even death on a cross. (Philippians 2.4–8)

This world values power. The power of wealth, the power of status, the power of influence. Jesus is asking his disciples to take up their cross and follow him, and says still to those who claim to be his followers that true greatness is found in pursuing the power of love and the emptying of self for the good of the other.

Response

Do you prefer Palm Sunday or Good Friday? Why?

We live in a world of political protest – what are the differences and similarities with the Palm Sunday crowd? Are there things we can learn from this story to help us in our own activism?

The message of Palm Sunday, the celebration of peace, is realized through the acceptance of the cross of Good Friday. What implications does this have for us, especially in the context of conflict?

Prayer

God of our journey,
you lead us through the green pastures
of Palm Sunday's hopeful celebration
when all is joyful and well-being assured.
You also lead through the valley of the shadow
of Good Friday
when loss casts a fearful shadow of pain and despair.
You rode the colt of peace
and hung on a cross of sacrifice
to demonstrate the power of love.
May we be transformed by that cross,
to follow you faithfully
in days of hope and nights of loss,
for you lead us as the God of peace
whose love has won all.
Amen.

Reflections for Holy Week and Easter

Holy Week – Years A, B and C

The same texts are set for the different days of Holy Week across all the years of the lectionary cycle. In this section there are reflections for each day from individual authors, including two for the Liturgy of the Passion which is sometimes used on Palm Sunday. There is also a themed set for the whole week, including Easter Day, which looks at the different types of space we see characters in the Passion narrative acting in, or out of.

Liturgy of the Passion Year A – Matthew 27.15–23

Janet Foggie

Introduction

The Passion reading for Year A is Matthew 26.14—27.66. Reading the whole story through several times might allow different aspects to come into clearer focus. Here we will look at the section 27.15–23 and explore ways in which jealousy enters the story of the crucifixion.

Envy is a particularly hard sin to define within ourselves – it is easy to see when another is jealous, or to ascribe envy as the motivation for another's actions, but very hard to see it within ourselves. This lack of ability to self-diagnose jealousy as a motivating factor is one of the reasons it is such a dangerous sin. We could see a jealousy of the other disciples in Judas' betrayal of Jesus: it is easy to read into his willingness to sell his Lord a perverted desire to love Jesus, expressed as a feeling of disappointment that he did not get as close to him as he wanted. When we are feeling jealous, and we are crossed, then human beings can be very dangerous indeed.

Have you ever felt jealous? What was the cause? How did it feel?

Is there a time you acted badly from a place of envy without realizing it? What were the consequences?

Do you see a difference between envy and jealousy? If so, how would you express that?

Comment

'For he knew that it was out of envy that they had delivered him up' (v. 18). Pilate has been able to see a truth in this situation that the Jewish leaders, Judas and the crowd cannot see. The enemy of the people, the foreign ruler and judge has seen a truth which is vital to understanding the whole picture of what is happening to Jesus. Crucially for the rest of the narrative though, Pilate does not share this knowledge.

Jealousy is a very difficult sin to name, partly because we are all guilty of it; it is a sin of degrees. It is also one that the person being envious is often blind to and yet that is very damaging to their self-esteem to name to them. When we accuse another person of being jealous, we bring them down twice: first because jealousy is a nasty thing to be accused of and second because we are opening up the reality that the jealous person is acting out of the belief that they lack something which another person has. To suggest openly, as leader of the Roman presence in Jerusalem, that the Jewish leaders might be jealous of Jesus, would be to suggest they compared themselves to Jesus and found themselves lacking.

Instead Pilate asks a different question: 'Whom do you want me to release for you, Barabbas or Jesus who is called Christ?' We don't know what the reply was at that moment because he is interrupted by a note of warning sent by his wife, who has had troubled dreams. This takes us back to stories of Joseph and Pharaoh and other interventions by women such as Esther or Sarah. However, this is not an Old Testament tale, and the note in this instance is to no avail.

It almost seems strange that it is mentioned at all, since Pilate's wife has no other role and features in the story in no other way. Perhaps it is evidence that Pilate had opportunities to think better of what he was doing. Or maybe it is simply mentioned because it happened – a note came into the room, a moment of tension was broken and those who might perhaps have been persuaded to think about their actions another way were able to regroup and argue for Christ's death. Often when people are acting badly, a pause can be uncomfortable as they feel that moment of unspoken criticism in the room – very rarely do we have no idea of the wrong we are committing, but when we are speaking, acting or nursing our own self-righteousness, we can suppress the thought.

It is very rare to meet a person who is knowingly jealous, and rarer still to meet someone who will admit to being a bully. People acting out of jealousy often use bullying behaviour to bring down the person who threatens them, the person they have judged to be better than themselves in some unreachable feature, and so to be a threat. The Jewish leaders could never accept that jealousy was the root motivation of their bullying. But the bullying itself is, oddly, to them, a justification that wipes out any hint of jealousy. The need to kill Jesus becomes an end in itself; motivation and causation are not discussed. The issues of 'guilt' or 'innocence' are not on the table. It is not that he has *done* something wrong and must be punished, but rather he *is* something wrong. His goodness is showing up their jealousy and petty envy and so cannot be tolerated. This is why there is no punishment for Jesus that is enough for the crowd – it is not his actions that are being corrected or balanced by a punishment fitting a crime, it is his personhood which is an affront, and so it must be obliterated.

Response

Reflect on a situation where you have been jealous. Can you identify how or where envy was at work? Have there ever been times when jealousy on your part has led to behaviour which others might feel was bullying? What can you do about that? What did you do then?

What are the antidotes to jealousy? A theology of personhood? An improved self-esteem? For some it is seeing faults in those we idolize, for others it is improving how we view ourselves. In his ministry on this earth, Jesus tended to expect his disciples to focus more on what they could change about themselves than on what they could change in others.

Prayer

God of all the injustices,
I never thought I was a jealous person
until I realized the envy I felt
and was moved by its power –
seeing that jealousy is strong enough
to send Christ to the cross
making me wonder at the force of my own sin.

I am sorry for my jealous thoughts.
I am sorry for my actions which stem from envy.
I am sorry for trying to take others down to my level.
Forgive me, merciful God,
Forgive me, Jesus, as you forgave
those who killed you in rage and jealousy
for they knew not what they did.

Thanks to you, gracious God,
who has made each human
unique, precious, a single individual
living in community, living in society,
of worth and of value
found in being, not in achievements or goals.
Gather me in, with all the souls you have created
into your holy presence which starts here on earth
and in heaven finds its never-ending purpose
of worshipful joy.
Amen.

Liturgy of the Passion Year B – Mark 15.1–15

Fiona Bullock

Introduction

Before we get to the joy of the resurrection, we must journey with Christ through some of his most difficult times. He is betrayed and rejected. He has a farewell meal with his disciples – who still don't understand when he tells them he will die soon. He is arrested and ridiculed by the Council and then viciously beaten. He is deserted and denied by his friends. Alone, beaten and tired, he faces Pilate, and later, the baying crowd. The voices are deafening but the place of silence is compelling.

As you read this excerpt from the Passion Sunday reading, where do you find the power and the vulnerability, the noise and the silence?

Comment

Voices, voices, voices! Everyone seems to have something to say. All I can hear is the noise in this passage. The chief priests are accusing. Pilate is asking questions. The crowds are shouting. No one knows what to do with this man Jesus but everyone has something to say. Voices, voices, voices!

As I read these words from Mark's Gospel, there is so much noise I can't hear my own thoughts. When they come, all I have done is added another voice into the mix and it all gets jumbled up. Voices, voices, voices!

Not long before, the crowds had gathered in many different places to hear Jesus' voice. They were desperate to hang on to every word he would offer about the kingdom of God. They needed to hear the assurance of God's love for them. They

sought forgiveness and compassion. They wanted together-
ness. As he spoke about how different life could be if only they
could put the last first and care for one another, they wanted
to believe that this could be true. Maybe then they would have
a voice and a place of belonging.

But there were other voices back then too. The authorities
spoke behind closed doors about the threat that this trouble-
maker posed and what they should do about him. The voice of
Judas betrayed his friend and master. The people of the crowd
were beginning to wonder if it was worth the hassle to follow
this strange man – were they really prepared to leave behind
the life they knew and follow him? Probably not.

Voices, voices, voices! So many voices. So many thoughts.
Like a tornado that picks you up, spins you around and won't
let you go.

In the middle of the whirlwind, there is Jesus. People accuse,
they ask, they jeer and Jesus says nothing. Does he stay silent
because he feels that they won't listen to him anyway? Does he
say nothing because he knows what will happen next? Or is he
simply speechless in the face of all the hate and fear and noise?
Voices, voices, voices!

In this story, through all the noise, I find myself drawn to
Jesus. He represents both my distress, as I listen to all the conflicting voices around me, and my comfort, as the quiet centre
of it all. I don't doubt that he is frustrated. After everything
he has said and done, after everything he has poured out of
himself, why is he alone in the midst of a crowd? Who is on his
side? When he no longer has a voice that will be heard, who
will speak up for him?

Yet, he is also the quiet centre in the storm of emotions. The
noise is deafening but he is the stillness. He calls to me in that
moment to be with him and to share the calm in the middle of
my turmoil. His silence allows me to hear his voice most clearly
in my heart. 'I love you as you are. I am with you.' He does not
clamour for my attention but he has it fully. I want to stand
there with him until my storm subsides, or I have to stand in its
eye and face its full force head on. It doesn't give me solutions

or responses to all the voices around me but I am reminded and reassured that I am not alone. There is power in a voice but the transformative power of silence can be awesome.

Response

- What are the people saying in your context today?
- Consider the power of a voice. Consider the power of silence. Which will you use today?
- During a time when you feel overwhelmed by the noise, stop and allow yourself to be drawn to the quiet centre we find in Jesus.

Prayer

God of our loneliness in the crowd
God of our silence in the noise
God of our calm in the storm,
help us to be,
and in our being, help us to love ourselves
and know the embrace
of your all-encompassing love.
Amen.

Monday of Holy Week – John 12.1–11

Fiona Bullock

Introduction

Jesus gave Lazarus life. He retrieved him from the darkness of his cavern tomb and brought him out into the light again. Those who saw believed, but there were some who immediately reported Jesus to the authorities. Threatened by Jesus, they plotted to kill him and Lazarus.

Having been brought back to life, Lazarus seems to disappear in today's passage. It is easy to fixate on Jesus, as the plans to end his life are made in the background. It is easy to be distracted by the actions of Mary or the indignation of Judas. Yet just as the great crowds came to see Jesus, they also, John tells us, came to see the risen Lazarus.

Pushed to the side, I wonder how Lazarus would tell his story. This imaginative reflection suggests ways to fill in the gaps. What does this change of perspective draw out of the story?

Comment

Every morning when I wake up, I pinch myself. I can't believe it's true. I have woken up, I'm alive! There are no cloths around my head and no stone over the entrance to the tomb. It's a miracle! I am a living miracle! I'm alive!

No one could believe it. My sisters have been fussing around me since it happened. I've noticed crowds gathering wherever I go and the pointing ... well, I'll never get used to that. Or the staring for that matter. I've always been used to being in the background. You have to – having sisters like mine – not that Mary means to take centre stage. It just happens; and Martha, always busy, always having people round – she's good at hospitality. They can't believe I'm alive again. I can't believe it either. I've got a second chance. An opportunity to do things differently or the same again. It's my choice.

Everyone thinks I should be really excited and grateful and I suppose I am. I should be ecstatic and raring to go but I'm sitting in a corner of this crowded room and after all the pointing and staring and questions, no one seems to have noticed that I've retreated. I've had my 15 minutes of fame and now it's all about the others. I don't want to be in the spotlight but what am I supposed to do with life part two?

Nobody tells you about that part. I feel so much pressure to get it right. Am I destined to live out the rest of my days with the label, 'Lazarus – the man Jesus raised from the dead' plastered to my forehead? Do I have to prove that it was worth Jesus taking the time to perform the miracle of raising me from the dead? Or am I just 'Lazarus – the brother of Martha and Mary'? What about me?

Does anyone know anything about me? Has anyone ever asked about my passion or my goals in life? No, the only time I matter is when I'm the living proof of a Jesus miracle.

They're out to get me, or so I heard. Some of the people pointing and staring want me dead. I am so scared. I don't want to die again, not yet, but right now, people are more scared that Jesus might be killed.

I'm going to sit here for a while. I wonder if anyone will notice I'm still here.

Response

- Sit with Lazarus for a while. How do you think he would tell his story?
- Think about a time when you felt like you had disappeared in a crowded room. How did it feel to be 'lost to view'?
- In the conflicts you experience, whose perspectives are being assumed without questions being asked?
- Watch out for others who retreat in other circumstances you find yourself in and reach out to them.

Prayer

'What was the point in raising me from the dead if I'm just to be ignored?'
'Why am I always working?'
'I can't believe he is going to die.'
'He makes me so angry letting her off the hook like that! That money could have been mine.'

Lord, we ask for your forgiveness,
for the times we have missed the point
or forgotten to think about others.
Help us to have the ability to see another's perspective
so we can learn to be gracious
or to graciously teach others.
Amen.

Tuesday of Holy Week – John 12.20–36
Brec Seaton

Introduction

What do we do when faced with a difficult situation in life? A time when we have a choice about how to respond, a time when that choice may lead to potentially different outcomes? Do we stay to face the situation and perhaps fight our corner? Do we run away as fast as possible without looking back? In this passage, Jesus makes such a choice – a choice that ultimately leads to his death. We read why this was his choice and that he saw that, through this, changes would occur that would bring goodness to both Jews and to those who were marginalized within society.[1]

Comment

The gospel passage just before our reading takes us to two extremes in how one man is perceived by those around him. On the one hand, following the raising of Lazarus, Jesus is the hero of the hour and the world is following him. And yet, at the same time, the Pharisees see Jesus as such a threat to their way of life that they plot to kill not only him but Lazarus too. Life can't get more dangerous than knowing there is a death warrant out for you – and Jesus appears to be well aware of his predicament.

Jesus momentarily considers calling for his father to rescue him, a possibility of running to a safe space, before clearly stating that, 'No – it is for this reason that I have come to this hour' (v. 27). We sense the inner turmoil of a man who knows what he has to do, but who would like this situation to be a million miles away. It is interesting that Jesus doesn't follow either of our natural instincts – he hasn't fled, but neither is he fighting for survival. He stays in the turmoil. How and why does he do this?

At the beginning of our passage (v. 20), we read that some Greeks had sought council with Jesus. We don't know why they were not able to go directly to Jesus, or if Jesus communicated directly with them, or even if they heard the words Jesus spoke. We don't know if they were Gentiles, or Jews living among the Gentiles. Yet this encounter prompted Jesus' next thoughts: 'A single grain must fall to the earth and die, in order for it to bear a lot of fruit – otherwise it stays as a single grain.' In replying to Philip and Andrew, Jesus is reminding himself of his mission – he had come for the salvation of all – Jews, Greeks and Gentiles. As he prepares for the turmoil of his death, Jesus is stating his mission to both himself and the world. Knowing that death will bring much fruit means Jesus doesn't try to fix, or manipulate, or fight, or run away. Jesus knows a new life will come that will bring transformation to many. In this short sentence, Jesus is sharing with us how he manages to stay in this place of inner turmoil – in order for new life to emerge.

Jesus encourages his listeners to take a risk – to lose your life in order to find a new life. He invites the crowd on to the journey, to take the opportunities that come when challenges arise and to be wise in this journey: 'walk while you have the light ... believe in the light'. The challenge is that we don't actually know what this new life will look like, what it will feel like, what we will experience, until we have journeyed through this space from one life to another. And to enter this space, we must first lay down all that is precious to us.

Response

How many of us, when faced with a very difficult situation of conflict, stay and fight the situation, and how many of us try to run away – as fast as we can – to our 'safe space'? How easy is it to stay and 'be' in this difficult place? How do we make the decision about what to do? Do we just react in the moment?

Do we seek refuge before moving towards the conflict? Do we seek the bigger picture? Do we 'sit' in the turmoil? What journey do we choose to make and how do we make that choice?

You are invited to find a space to sit in that is free from distraction, with some paper and coloured pencils. Consider for a moment what are the most precious things in your life – and write or draw images to represent these.

Now consider which of these precious areas of your life draw you closer to who you truly are before God. Mark these in a different coloured pencil. Which of these precious areas of your life have the potential to be a barrier between yourself and God? Mark these in a different coloured pencil.

In the quiet and solitude, allow God to speak to you. What is God saying about what is precious in your life? What is God saying about losing your life in order to save it?

Prayer

When we are in deep pain and life has taken a fall –
let us know you are near.
When we struggle to get out of bed and face the world –
let us feel you close by.
When all around us the world is carrying on as though all
    is well –
let us be immersed in your love.
When we are unable to love ourselves, let alone those who
    are close to us –
Let your arms wrap around us and hold us tight …

And when we emerge from our time of turmoil,
when we have wrestled and rested in our liminal space and
    found you,
when we have crossed to a place that we never dreamt of –
let the seed that was buried for so long rise up and bear fruit.
Let the fruit of that seed be a blessing
to those who journeyed with us in our turmoil,
to those who are in pain and despair,

to those who we meet each day,
to the stranger we only meet once.

May the peace we find be infectious,
may the peace we find be passed on to others.
May the peace we inhabit
be always found in you
as we live in the joy
of your everlasting love.
Amen.

Note

1 See Lent 5B for another reflection on this text (p. 153).

Wednesday of Holy Week – John 13.21–32

Brec Seaton

Introduction

Our passage falls at an interesting time in the reading of John's Gospel. Immediately prior, Jesus takes the role of a servant to his disciples, washing their feet. Immediately after, he becomes an authority figure, telling them what they must do – love one another. In between, we see an apprehensive Jesus foretelling his own betrayal.

The passage captures Jesus troubled in spirit, the disciples misunderstanding and misreading the situation, a contradiction, and issues of power and powerlessness.

Comment

Picture the scene: a low table with seating on the floor; the remnants of a shared meal. John – full, relaxed and reclining after the meal. Jesus, in contrast, is anxious and troubled – trying to savour this one last taste of normality among close friends before the torture, pain and humiliation that is to come – he is not relaxed or reclining. His spirit in turmoil and unable to keep his feelings to himself any longer, he says, 'I tell you, one of you will betray me' (v. 21). Jesus has already hinted at this with his earlier comment that, 'you are clean, though not all of you' (v. 10). Did the disciples not pick this up? The two comments play on Simon Peter's mind and he finally motions to John to find out more and he asks Jesus, 'Lord, who is it?' (v. 25).

The disciples do not understand what Jesus is really getting at. He has given them a riddle and they need to see the picture through a different lens to begin to understand. They don't do this and assume that Judas is going out to do a job he is assigned to do on behalf of this group of friends. Did Simon Peter not wonder how Judas was going to betray Jesus, or why? Or did he assume he had misunderstood and that no betrayal was going to take place – after all, they had been a close group for three years now.

How often do we fall into this trap of making wrong assumptions? We see life through the lens of our experiences, our expectations and our hopes. Peter looked at Judas and heard the words of Jesus through his own experiences and expectations. He didn't consider the real reason why Judas was leaving the room – even though Jesus had just spelt out what was to happen. Jesus' reaction to the disciples' assumptions, as recorded in John's Gospel, is in sharp contrast to an earlier interaction with Nicodemus. Nicodemus, a teacher of the law, seeks to find out how to enter the kingdom of God and is effectively told off by Jesus for not understanding (John 3.10) Yet Jesus does not reprimand the disciples for their lack of understanding, neither does he correct their wrong assumptions – there seems to be an interesting contradiction between how Jesus reacts to this deficiency in his own group of disciples, and in a Pharisee. Yet in some ways the former seems a worse thing.

Simon Peter made a choice in finding out who would betray Jesus. He then made a choice in how to respond to the reply – he chose to be a bystander. Rather than continue to ask more questions and find out Judas' intentions, he appears to have done nothing. The term 'Bystander Effect' was popularized in the 1960s when a group of people observed a murder in New York City but did not step in to assist or call the police. Social psychologists Bibb Latané and John Darley attributed the bystander effect to two things: the perceived diffusion of responsibility (onlookers are more likely to intervene if there are few or no other witnesses) and social influence (individuals in a group monitor the behaviour of those around them to determine how to act).[1]

Was the fact that Peter was in a group, and that no one else asked any questions of Jesus, critical in this lack of further action from Peter? It would appear that Peter felt powerless to act further – through lack of understanding and making assumptions, and in being part of a larger group whose behaviour didn't reinforce or back up his initial question. From John's account it would appear that not one of the disciples tried to stop Judas from leaving their company that evening. Peter had not felt able to directly ask Jesus who would betray him and now feels powerless to ask more questions before Judas leaves.

Judas leaves the room on Jesus' command – after receiving bread that Jesus had dipped in the dish – an act reserved for deep friendship and, in the light of what is to happen, a contradiction in the use of this act. We read that it was night and presumably therefore dark. It is a theme we see throughout John's writing – the contrast between light and dark. Did John say it was night because of the spiritual turmoil that Jesus was feeling? Yet darkness only exists because of light and light because of darkness – the interdependence of this metaphor must not be lost – for the whole of this passage is one of interdependence. Indeed, the utter darkness and rejection that Jesus feels just a few hours later is interdependent on the magnificent resurrection and glorification of the Son of God that is to come just a few days later.

Response

We can all be in situations where we feel helpless, with a sense of having no power to act to change a situation. Sometimes all we can do is to be in the mess of life, sitting with one another and journeying through the ugly. The gospel reading is right at the beginning of this most difficult and painful time for Jesus and his friends and family. John invites us to journey through the darkness until one day the light breaks through once again. This time with the deep wounds, the disruptions, the cracks, changes how the light is reflected from us and back into the world.

We can also be in situations where, like Peter and the disciples, we choose not to act to change a situation, to look away, or accept an explanation that allows us to stifle our disquiet. How can we be more aware of when we are doing this? What steps can we take to act differently in such situations?

The Corrymeela Community have an excellent free resource called 'BYstanding' – a series of short films with an educators' guide – which looks at this issue in the context of sectarianism in Northern Ireland.[2]

Prayer

God of the troubled heart –
you call us to journey in the dark places of life
you call us to journey in the hard places of life
you call us to journey with those who struggle
you call us to sit in the mess of life
unable to put things right.

In these times, God
may our thoughts be a prayer to you
may our words be of hope and understanding
may our actions be a response to your love for us
may our very being bring light to those who are in darkness.
Amen.

Notes

1 See more on the Bystander Effect at www.psychologytoday.com/basics/bystander-effect.

2 Further information can be found on their website: www.corrymeela.org.

Maundy Thursday – John 13.1–7, 31b–35

Trevor Williams

Introduction

Yesterday, we read of Judas leaving the 'last supper' to facilitate the arrest of Jesus. 'And it was night.' That story is placed between verses 7 and 31b of today's reading. It is worth noting that Jesus' demonstration of self-giving love for his disciples is in the turmoil of imminent betrayal, impending suffering and an unknown future.

There is no clearer portrayal of what it means to be a follower of Jesus than to be, above all, a foot washer!

What are the essential attributes of an effective leader?

Preparation

Think of a time you were given a generous gift, far beyond what was expected – how did you respond? What was behind that response?

Comment

On this Maundy Thursday, when we think of the last supper, and when we remember that it was on this evening that Jesus said, 'Do this in remembrance of me', let us for a moment look at this sacrament of forgiveness and new life which Jesus has given us, through the story of the foot washing.

Jesus, in the middle of this solemn meal, gets up from the table, takes off his outer garment and then, dressed only in a flimsy tunic (which could go down to the knees or the ankles and was possibly sleeveless), he fills a basin of water. What is he at? Jesus puts a towel around his waist and bends down and starts washing the feet of his disciples.

He comes eventually to Peter – and there he meets resistance! Like many of us, Peter instinctively believes in hierarchy. There are important people at the top and there are unimportant people at the bottom. Peter is quite prepared to wash the feet of Jesus. But it's just not right the other way around. What would we do if Jesus came to our house and offered to tidy up the kitchen and do the washing up? And then says he might as well clean the toilets. We'd probably react in the same way as Peter.

Jesus then says something very strange: 'If I cannot wash your feet, you shall have no part of me.' Very strong words – 'If I cannot wash your feet, you cannot share in the kingdom.'

This kingdom is a contrast culture where service, not success, is the measure of life; where people are valued not for who or what they are, but simply because they are children of God.

This is the only time that Jesus says, 'I have done this as an example ... So if I, your Lord and Teacher, have washed your feet, you also ought to wash one another's feet.'

Imagine yourself sitting among the disciples. Jesus now comes to you. He kneels. Takes the sandal gently off your foot and pours on the refreshing water. How does it feel that Jesus is washing your feet? Are you uncomfortable? Maybe you're more comfortable giving than receiving from others. Do you deserve this intimate act of caring from Jesus? You haven't been the person you know you should have been – and this act of washing your feet makes you feel terribly exposed for who you are. Maybe you want to be 'left alone' like Peter rather than face what has surfaced through this act of loving service. But Jesus insists ...

This act of service shows that you are loved, accepted as you are. There is no need to hide, to cloak the past – it is all fully known. No need to pretend you are better than you are – you are loved, warts and all. You are accepted. That is what the forgiveness of Jesus means.

Jesus' ability to forgive was amazing. On the cross he said, 'Father, forgive them, for they do not know what they do.' The

Croatian theologian Miroslav Volf has said that forgiveness needs a kind of double vision – an ability to move beyond your own pain and put yourself into the shoes of the perpetrator. To see things from their point of view. Jesus is, in that cry from the cross, saying, 'I can see it from their point of view, they don't understand. Forgive them, Father.'

At Corrymeela's centre at Ballycastle we have worship twice a day, which guests are invited to attend if they want to. On one occasion, towards the end of a residential programme, some members of a youth group turned up for what was to be their last worship. At the end of the very simple form, as people sat in a circle around a lighted candle, a cross and a Bible, the young people were asked if they wished to pray for anybody who they were concerned about. One young person said, 'I would like to pray for a man. He is in prison tonight. He is very worried. His wife, children and family are worried because tomorrow he returns to court to be sentenced.' After the worship, this young girl was asked who it was that she had wanted prayer for – who was this man in prison? She said, 'He's the man who murdered my father.'

This girl had double vision. She could feel the anxiety of this man and his family. That moved her. Even though this man was the cause of such pain.

Jesus had double vision. When from the cross he said, 'Father, forgive', he looked around at those responsible, the religious leaders, the crowds shouting crucify, he looks at you and me – caught up in and contributing to the sinful web of the world – and he says, 'Father, forgive them, they do not know what they are doing.'

How is this possible – this double vision; this possibility to find space, in our suffering, to recognize the suffering of others? That space, that double vision, is possible when we have a sense that we are forgiven: we love because he first loved us; we forgive because we are forgiven.

So how can we contribute to reconciliation? We have an opportunity every time we receive communion – the tokens of Christ, given up for us. In receiving this, in acceptance of Christ washing our feet, offering us forgiveness, we take another step on the journey towards wholeness. And in finding that inner peace, we have more room to undertake the costly task of forgiving others. When we know we are forgiven, then we can forgive others. When we are served with love, we learn how to serve. When we are loved as Jesus loves, then we can love others as he did.

Response

When you find it just too difficult to live in harmony with God's coming kingdom, what in this scripture passage might be able to support you?

Is there someone you find difficult to forgive? Why is it difficult? Is there something you can do in response to this passage?

Prayer

Shocking God,
you turn our world upside down!
Shock us into new life,
that your loving-kindness
may resonate through
our thoughts, words and deeds,
and our lives reflect
the generosity of Jesus' love.
Amen.

Good Friday – John 18.1—19.42

Trevor Williams

Introduction

Good Friday and Easter morning are inseparable. They belong to a single event whose impact has changed history, is capable of changing how we see our world, our life, our future.

Numerous theories have arisen to explain why God allowed an innocent man to die like this.

I suggest today that we don't debate the theory, we simply hear the story of Good Friday and allow that story to speak to us of God's love for us and for our world. As you stand at the foot of the cross, this is an opportunity to see what it means for you now. It is an old story and there can be nothing new in it. Yet today is different from all other days. And you are attending to that story in the unique circumstances of your life just now, with today's joys and sorrows, today's hopes and fears, today's achievements and failures. Give time today to hear afresh the Good Friday story.

Comment

'He said to his mother, "Woman, here is your son." Then he said to the disciple, "Here is your mother." And from that hour the disciple took her into his own home.'

In committing his mother and his disciple to support each other, Jesus affirms what has always been his priority – relationships. What matters in our life is not the size of the bank balance, not the size of our house, but the quality of our relationships. This is the true currency of life.

But the quality of intimacy that is pictured here is not just for family, for those next to us, or even for those like us. It embraces the thief on the cross, even our enemy. Love your enemy, says Jesus. Love is the hallmark of the Christian life and what it means to follow Jesus. We have seen already how Jesus loves, the extent to which he forgives and the types of people whom he befriends – sinners, down and outs, those whom any 'decent' person wouldn't associate with. Jesus encompasses those people with his love. And in receiving his love, marvellous things happen. They find new life.

Jesus' extraordinary life was an illustration of the message he preached. It was always about the kingdom of God, the kingdom of right relationships. It was passion for God's will to be done on earth as it is in heaven that brought Jesus into confrontation with the temple authorities and finally led to his crucifixion. As followers of Jesus, we are also called to live this alternative lifestyle where peace is the alternative to violence; inclusion the alternative to the emergence of elites; the sharing of goods the alternative to amassing wealth; where a God of the powerless is the alternative to a God who sanctions inequalities. As Jesus lived, so he died – caring first and foremost for right relationships.

'After this ... he said, "I am thirsty."' Jesus is quoting Psalm 69: 'Save me, O God ... I am weary with my crying; my throat is parched. My eyes grow dim with waiting for my God ...'

Why, out of all the physical abuse of the cross, is thirst singled out? Well, this is John's Gospel – the one in which Jesus asks the Samaritan woman for a drink and tells her 'but those who drink of the water that I will give them will never be thirsty' (John 4.13–14). So this is another dimension of what is missing when Jesus says, 'I thirst': Christ continues to long for the coming of God's kingdom; the liberation of all creation. Here on Good Friday, we see the marshalling of all the evil powers of this world against the Son of God and we see their total destructiveness exemplified in the suffering of Christ. When the love of God meets sin, there is suffering. God suffers, for God is love.

Sin includes the attitudes or prejudices, ways of acting or behaving, that destroy others rather than build them up, that break right relationships rather than restore peace. Sin is opposition to the kingdom of God, the kingdom of right relationships. God gave humanity a special place in his creation: power to be the stewards of creation, to care for and nurture the life of all things and all people. But this God-given power has been misused – instead we have used power to dominate and exploit others for our gain; to mine the earth's wealth to extinction, disrupting the balance of nature by our insatiable desire to consume; we have used the power of violence to pursue our selfish desires.

We collude with world systems of domination which emanate from the love of power rather than the power of love. Domination of economic and political power, through violence if necessary, is accepted as the way to achieve security. We see these domination systems on the news every night. And these systems are so powerful, they hold us in their grip. They enslave us in patterns of living which are totally contrary to the kingdom of God.

Jesus was put to death by these powers – crucifixion was a key way in which authorities in the ancient world demonstrated their power to subjected peoples and broke the spirit of any resistance. The power of domination. Jesus refused to compromise or to join in their violent power games and died as he lived – committed to the kingdom of God, to God's will for the good of all creation, loving, caring and suffering for the good of others.

'Jesus said, "It is accomplished."'

This was not just the end of suffering – Jesus had fulfilled his God-given mission: remaining faithful from the baptism in the Jordan to crucifixion at Golgotha.

Could the cross have been avoided? Only if Christ compromised on his message, his life, his work, his relationship with God the Father. That was not an option. He refused to retaliate, to meet violence with violence. That's the way of the world. At his trial he refused to answer trumped-up accusations and false representations. He accepted, absorbed the evil violence of the powerful and in so doing neutralized it. This was a cry of joy, of victory – completing the work he had been sent to do without wavering, without denying the way, the truth and the life God had given him.

On Easter morning, the world saw that Jesus was vindicated by God. Jesus showed that the greatest power in the world wasn't the systems of domination, superstates, the powerful economic and political forces, the culture of 'self first' that drives our consumerist culture, disregards justice and dismisses love as irrelevant. Instead, as his life and death have shown, the greatest power in our world is God's love. The powers were defeated on the cross. They had done their worst and ultimately failed.

Response

How is the story of Good Friday a source of hope for you?

It is in returning to the story of Jesus' passion and resurrection that we are renewed in God's love. How do you keep this story central to your life? What helps you? What distracts you?

Are you convinced that the greatest power in the world is the love of God? How may that reality change your perspective on events that trouble you?

Prayer

Thanks be to you, our Lord Jesus Christ,
for all the benefits which you have given us,
for all the pains and insults which you have borne for us.
Most merciful Redeemer, Friend and Brother,
may we know you more clearly,
love you more dearly,
and follow you more nearly, day by day.
Amen.[1]

Note

1 Richard, Bishop of Chichester (1197–1253).

Good Friday – John 18.1—19.42

Sarah Hills

Introduction

We have been journeying through Lent and Holy Week and now arrive at Good Friday. Every Holy Week is a difficult journey. We come from Palm Sunday, with its hope of triumph and celebration, through the inexorable progress towards the cross. Jesus and his friends, his companions, travelled together towards the Passover, faint 'Hosannas' ringing in their ears as they sat at the table together in the upper room. The journey to the cross is a journey of many things – disappointment, confusion, misunderstanding, fear, love. It is also a journey of relationship. Conflicts are often portrayed by extremes, or by using catastrophic language. 'I hate you.' 'I wish you were dead.' 'They are the worst people in the world.' But conflicts are also beset by and consist of more ordinary, less extreme feelings. Bewilderment. Disappointment. Misunderstanding. These won't kill or maim, but they nevertheless mark the path of the conflict journey. We ignore them at our peril.

Preparation

As we prepare to read John's telling of Jesus' last journey, let us think about relationships in the light of these more 'ordinary' emotions that we may ourselves be very familiar with – disappointment, confusion, misunderstanding. Jesus and Judas. Simon Peter. Thomas. Philip. The other Judas (not Iscariot). The disciples. And as we think about those relationships, let's also think about our own relationships this Holy Week in the light of these same emotions – disappointment, confusion, misunderstanding. Because these are the emotions that have been around all year during this pandemic and may have

beset many of our relationships. As we read John's account of
Good Friday, let us acknowledge with the disciples the depth
of confusion, misunderstanding and disappointment we may
feel already. Emotions ripe for fresh conflict to erupt.

Comment

There are many lenses we can use to reflect on this reading.
I'm going to focus on the relationships we find and the journey these relationships take. Conflict is always contextual and
where the relations are played out also matters. Whose was the
land we are fighting over and who wants it next?

The context on Good Friday for Jesus and those he was in
relationship with over those last hours was played out over a
physical journey as well as a relational one. We are taken from
a garden of violence to a hill of crucifixion. A long difficult
journey of only hours. It is a journey in which the emotions of
confusion, misunderstanding and disappointment are heightened further. A journey in which relationships turn sour and
emotions become extreme. Judas betrays Jesus. Simon Peter
uses violence and then betrayal. Pilate asks one of the most
crucial questions ever, 'What is truth?' before, against his own
judgement, letting the crowd have their way. Jesus is mocked,
tortured and executed.

There is a poem by the thirteenth-century Persian poet Rumi
in which he writes, 'Out there beyond ideas of wrong doing
and right doing, there is a field. I'll meet you there.'

As we journey through the relationships that were played
out on Good Friday, I'd like us to imagine this field – the field
of meeting beyond wrong or right doing. What do you imagine
this field to be like? Just take a moment to think about your
field – where is it and who are you going to meet there?

The field you are thinking about now might be a place of
childhood memories; of playing in a meadow; the field might
be a field of gold; or it might be a muddy field, shell pocked,
fought over, in Passchendaele; or a field of scorched earth in
Vietnam; a desert in South Sudan; Iraq, Syria, Israel/Palestine ...

Our field could be this desolate wounded place. It could be. It sometimes, it often is. On Good Friday it certainly was. And as we see from the meetings, the relationships that were already in place or new over that Good day, the journey to the field of the cross involved others who were not the ones we had hoped to be there. With one exception – that painfully tender meeting between Jesus, his mother Mary and John. 'Woman, here is your son.' And, 'Here is your mother.' The other meetings, relationships old or new, involved misunderstanding, confusion, disappointment, and gave way to the extremes of mockery, hate, violence, murder.

Looking at Jesus' journey through Good Friday and his relationships from the garden to the hill enables us to enter with him ultimately into that field beyond wrong and right doing. To meet 'the other'. This journey requires the one emotion we haven't seen much of so far in this journey. Love. Even love for our enemies in our field. Our field is a fundamental part of our journey. And maybe it is this field where Jesus was heading that day. The field beyond good or bad; friend or foe; perpetrator or victim. The love he showed from the cross despite, because of, everything.

Response

What is your field like? And who are you going to meet there? And where does our journey with Jesus take us today in the twenty-first century? In our own lives? In this time of Covid-19 conflict?

And who will we be open enough to meet in our field? In today's world, where white gated communities trump cardboard shacks; where Europe is again being torn apart; where the colour of your skin, or your gender, or your ethnicity, or your sexuality, can deny you justice; where your fields have been appropriated, or taken away, like those of the Canadian indigenous peoples and countless others around the world.

Prayer

Jesus
you were silent
in the face of Pilate's question.
May we too
not rush first
to build more constricting prisons
but instead
with the simplicity of a child
always look
for more holes in the sky.
Amen.[1]

Note

1 Prayer imagery based on a poem by Louis MacNeice in *Holes in the Sky Poems 1944–1947* (London: Faber and Faber, 1948).

Holy Saturday – John 19.38–42

Trevor Williams

Introduction

Holy Saturday is the day between. Jesus has been crucified and is dead. What now?

Practical tasks are to be done – arrange the burial, find a tomb, embalm the body. The practical tasks provide a brief distraction from emotional turmoil for two of Jesus' disciples, Joseph of Arimathea and Nicodemus.

But after the enormity of what has happened on Friday – the betrayal, the injustice of the trial, the extreme violence of the execution of one you not only knew but loved (how could it yet be 'Good' Friday?) – there is terror mixed with numbed confusion and a consuming sense of failure. Is this the end? The end of a promise of a new future? The end of hope?

For Jesus' disciples, trauma pervades Holy Saturday.

Comment

Two characters come into the open in today's reading: Joseph of Arimathea and Nicodemus. Both have been secret disciples. But on this Holy Saturday they are centre stage.

Joseph of Arimathea is mentioned in other gospels as 'a rich man and a disciple of Jesus' (Matthew 27.57); 'a respected member of the council (Sanhedrin), who was also himself looking for the kingdom of God' (Mark 15.43) and Luke adds that Joseph had 'not consented to (the Council's) decision and action' to demand the crucifixion of Jesus (Luke 23.50–56).

Nicodemus is mentioned three times in John's Gospel. He came to Jesus 'by night', acknowledging that Jesus was 'a teacher who has come from God; for no one can do these signs that you do apart from the presence of God' (John 3.2). The second mention is when the Pharisees were seeking to arrest Jesus and he protests that Jesus should be given a chance to defend himself. Nicodemus says, 'Our law does not judge people without first giving them a hearing to find out what they are doing, does it?' (John 7.50, 51). And in today's reading he brings spices – expensive spices that would typically be used for royalty – and together, Joseph and Nicodemus prepare the body and place it in the tomb.

Here were two men who belonged to that part of the contemporary Jewish religious and social system that was most criticized by Jesus and was fiercely opposed to everything Jesus stood for. Yet these two were secret disciples of Jesus.

Both Joseph and Nicodemus were caught between their group, as defined by their social status, religious calling, educational qualifications and work colleagues, and their curiosity about this young rabbi Jesus who, they recognized, had a ring of truth about him. For them, Jesus was an important messenger from God – but that was something that was better kept quiet. Until now!

They had been dismayed at the growing antagonism of their colleagues towards Jesus. They could hardly believe how things had come about – the spiral of violence growing deeper and wider until the crowds were shouting, 'Crucify!'

And now it was too late. Their attempts to persuade their colleagues to see reason and open their minds to what Jesus was about had failed. Now there was work to be done. Jesus, the person they respected, admired and secretly followed, could not be left on the cross to be thrown into a criminal's burial pit. If he had suffered an unjust trial and was an innocent victim of a tortuous crucifixion, they could at least give him a proper burial.

First, they had to risk asking for the removal of the body. That request would declare to the world that they were disciples of Jesus; their secrecy would no longer protect them. But for Joseph and Nicodemus, this was the moment of truth and they could not sit on the fence.

Having decided to make a stand, things became much clearer for them. Now they could express their devotion to Jesus not just by what they said, but by what they were about to do. Jesus deserved not just a decent burial, but a burial worthy of a king, with all the appropriate religious rituals carefully and lovingly observed.

So they embalmed Jesus' body and laid his body in the tomb.

Response

Holy Saturday is a quiet day. A day to take in the enormity of the events of Good Friday. How will you spend today?

Looking back to Friday, charged with negative emotions from the betrayal by a friend, the desertion by closest followers, the anger of the crowd, the skullduggery of political and religious leaders, the barbaric violence of death by crucifixion: how do you deal with negative emotions? How do you respond as you engage again with the events of Good Friday? Are there resonances here with difficult situations you are involved in? In the space of Holy Saturday, is there an insight to be gained?

Are there situations where you feel, or have felt, caught between conflicting allegiances? Are there any insights from this story which might help you engage with these dissonances or tensions?

Prayer

Jesus,
on this in-between day
when you were no longer visible
your disciples and friends were left
in the grip of strong emotions
and difficult choices.

Be with us in our in-between places
and whatever we are facing
may we know your constant presence with us
even if you are hidden from our sight.
Amen.

Holy Week – 'The Spaces We Inhabit'

These reflections for Holy Week form a thematic set and also include a reflection for the Resurrection of the Lord for Year A as part of this.

Introduction to the Set

Pat Bennett

One consequence of the restrictions to movement and contact during the pandemic has been to call our attention to things which often go unheeded – such as the physical, mental and emotional spaces we inhabit – or to things that we take for granted, such as human touch and interaction. This in turn has suggested a particular attentive focus for reading these familiar passages. An important but often overlooked element in conflict situations are the particular spaces – be those narrative, psychological, emotional, religious, historical, etc. – that people are inhabiting and the ways in which these can shape how they think and act, in both positive and negative ways. Stories of conflict and change are often also stories of people trapped by, or moving into, different spaces and the consequences of this – and this is something we also see in the densely packed stories of Holy Week.

Hence, these reflections for Holy Week and Easter in Year B will be looking at the different types of spaces – intense, contested, questioning, unsettling, profound and paradoxical, relational, courageous and disrupted – that the various characters occupy; and at how attention to these can help us to deepen our understanding of conflict and our responses to it.

Monday of Holy Week – John 12.1–11
'Intense space and contested space'

Pat Bennett

Introduction

This first reading for Holy Week brings us to one of the best known and best loved of the Passion vignettes – Mary anointing the feet of Jesus. This story, with its dramatic and evocative detail, has at its heart two very different spaces which overlap with one another.[1]

Preparation

Read through verse 3 and verse 5 several times and then try and capture the essence of each of them in one of the following ways: using the word 'perfume', make an acrostic describing Mary's actions or attitudes and then do the same for Judas; write a cinquain (a five-line poem with the structure noun/two adjectives/three verbs/two adverbs/noun) to capture what you feel is the essence of each verse; make a collage representing each verse using pictures and/or textured materials.

Comment

The most obvious space here is the one occupied by Jesus and Mary, which is created by her actions and his acceptance of them. There have been various different ways of reading this: as an act of prophetic witness foreshadowing Jesus' death or proclaiming his kingship; as an embarrassing incident which is at best immodest and at worst uncomfortably close to erotic; as a beautiful and intimate act of love and devotion; even as primarily something that Jesus does for Mary – accepting an action which implicitly elevates her above the disciples and even John the Baptist (who held himself 'not worthy to untie the thong of [Jesus'] sandal').

Our focus here though is not the quantitative meaning of the moment but its qualitative feel. Whatever Mary's motives were (which, in marked contrast to his treatment of Judas, John does not specify), what is absolutely clear is the intense quality which is the hallmark of this intimate space. John conveys this through the adjectives he uses – 'costly', 'pure' – and by the details of Mary's actions which he chooses to describe. This is not some neutral act of ritual hospitality, it is profoundly, intimately and emotionally connectional. Inevitably there is an overspill – no one is unaffected by the intensity of the moment – and intensity can be a two-edged sword, beautiful and dangerous! Just as the fragrance of the nard penetrates every corner of the house, so the effects of Mary's act also spread far beyond the two people caught up in it.

One of those ripple-out effects reveals a different space within the story, one which now also includes Judas. The hallmark of this space is a tension of a different kind and it is shaped, not by an action, but by the antagonism of a contested narrative. Once again there are various different ways of reading elements of this – particularly the enigmatic comments that Jesus makes about the poor. However, the key thing I want to attend to here is the way in which this moment which we have just witnessed is read in very different ways by those present.

What John's economical retelling shows us is that the intentions and actions at the centre of the story are interpreted and used in very different ways – and thus with correspondingly different consequences – by different characters within it. For Mary and, it seems, for Jesus, the anointing is both beautiful and deeply appropriate; for Judas (and the other disciples too, according to the synoptic accounts), it is wasteful and woefully misplaced. On the one hand it is an action that brings *shālôm*, on the other an action that implicitly causes its disruption by denying aid to those in need. We could also say that John himself uses the incident to service two very different narratives – one to do with the identity of Jesus and one with establishing (for whatever reason) a certain character for Judas.

So this first station on our Holy Week journey presents us with two things to reflect on with respect to conflict. First, that any situation which is highly charged – for whatever reason – will, like a stone dropped into a pool, set off a wave packet which spreads out far beyond the central point. We might therefore want to reflect on our own responses in situations of conflict and on the extent to which we are willing or able to regulate these to avoid amplifying or widening potential fall-out. Are there tools or techniques we can learn which will help us to be more aware of our own emotions and of when and how we might need to 'put a damper' on them?

Second, there is very rarely a simple narrative or a single set of understandings around any situation, particularly ones which involve conflict. What seems to us to be an obvious reading of a situation or delineation of its consequences, may appear very differently to another person directly involved or looking on. How, then, can we develop our awareness of what shapes our own readings of a particular conflict situation and critically examine these? How can we be more ready to hear and receive the narrative of the Other and give to that a properly critical, rather than simply prejudiced, attention?

Response

Go back to whichever task you did in preparation and revisit the different 'situation captures' you made for Mary and for Judas. Reflect on what prompted you to read the situation and respond in the way that you did. Is there anything here which you can take to help you reflect on a conflict situation (great or small, public or private) that you are currently involved in?

Alternatively, reflect on an intense situation you've been involved in. Were there ways in which your own responses had consequences beyond yourself or the immediate situation? With hindsight, is there anything you might have done differently in regulating those responses? Are there practices you could adopt which might help you if a similar situation arises?

Prayer

Jesus, the anointed one,
you were no stranger
to strong emotions
in yourself or others,
nor to the consequences
which sometimes
come in their train.

Help us to learn the discipline
of holding our emotions in check
when that is necessary,
and the freedom
to give them expression
when that is what is needed
for the health and comfort
of others and ourselves.
Amen.

Note

1 For a different lens on this text see the reflections for Lent 5C (p. 182).

Tuesday of Holy Week – John 12.20–36
'Questioning space'

Pat Bennett

Introduction

Today's passage holds some well-known and well-loved verses but overall can be somewhat perplexing, especially when read without its surrounding context. This feeling, though, is very apposite: the passage is punctuated by a number of questions but, as is so often the case, they don't necessarily receive answers; and even when they do, they don't always make things clearer![1]

Preparation

Read through the story and identify any questions that are raised in it. For each one, try and summarize, as succinctly as possible, what the question is about and the answer which is given (or not!). Finally, give a one- or two-word description of how the answer is received or the effect it has.

Comment

There are three distinct 'questioning spaces' in this passage. Each one is a little different and thus offers a different lens on the dynamics of conflict and our responses to it.

The first comes right at the start of the story. It appears as a request from 'some Greeks' who want to 'see Jesus' but clearly holds some implicit questions: 'How do we get to do that? Can you arrange it for us?' We never learn if they actually achieved their wish – instead we see Philip going to consult Andrew and the pair of them then approaching Jesus. His response to them mixes the cryptic, the poetic and the challenging in equal measure, but the Greek inquirers themselves are no more seen or heard from. We don't know why they made their request – perhaps they had heard about the raising of Lazarus, or had seen and been intrigued or mystified by Jesus' manner of entering Jerusalem – but it seems reasonable to suppose that what they actually want to do is to learn or understand a little more about who this person actually is.

Jesus begins by alluding to his forthcoming 'glorification' – a theme that is echoed and amplified by the thunderous voice from heaven in verse 28. In John's Gospel, the language of glory plays a key role in the way in which God and his purposes are made known through the actions of Jesus and in how the true identity of Jesus himself is gradually revealed. What then follows in the next ten verses, while somewhat enigmatic in places, is part of this unfolding of identity and purpose. So we might say that Jesus does indeed answer their enquiry – not by responding to the overt request, but by attending to the deeper questions and intentions which lie beneath its surface.

In the middle of this answer though, we encounter our second 'questioning space': suddenly Jesus breaks off and turns aside to ask a question *of himself*. It is almost as though he suddenly 'hears' what it is he is saying to those nearby and this provokes an inward tremor – 'Now my soul is troubled' – and an accompanying internal debate. We cannot know what is going on in his mind at this moment, but it feels almost as though he is reaching for a touchstone – perhaps something forged through his own journey – to steady his own sense of identity and purpose. Jesus then himself asks a question couched as a request and a voice from heaven responds as though (despite the subsequent comment in verse 30) to reinforce the answer which Jesus has already given himself to his earlier question.

The moment – though profound – passes quickly in John's account and Jesus returns to his explanatory answer, which leads us to our final space shaped by questions. Not only do those listening apparently fail to recognize the voice from heaven for what it is, but Jesus' subsequent comments merely produce a very disconcerting disjunction for them between the image of 'the Son of Man' they would have been familiar with from the writings of Daniel and Enoch and the one Jesus presents to them through his talk of loss and death. Their subsequent questions – 'How can you say that the Son of Man must be lifted up? Who is this Son of Man?' – reveal the jarring discord of an overturned world view. Jesus' response is not to provide a direct answer to these questions but to invite them to move forward, guided not by concrete answers but by something less tangible – a light which will, if they let it, allow them to begin to see, understand and become part of the different patterns of God's kingdom.

Questions are an intrinsic element of any conflict situation – but questions come in many different guises and serve many different purposes. Today's story presents us with just three of many possibilities to consider:

First, questions may not always be what they appear on the surface – and likewise answers may in fact be addressing what is hidden, or what the answerer believes to be hidden within them. Do we take the time to think about questions before we plunge into answering them? Do we routinely have a critical check on the assumptions we make which may drive our answers? And, from the other side of the coin, do we take time to consider what may lie behind the answers we are given, rather than going with our immediate response to these (which can often be very emotion-driven)?

Second, we need to take time to ask *ourselves* questions – particularly ones about our own sense of identity or the narratives by which we orientate our actions. We have touched before on the issue of the 'blind spots' which we all have and of the value of sometimes exploring these areas with the help of a trained listener or a trusted friend.

Finally, are we too dependent on having watertight answers, or fully developed understandings about situations before we can allow ourselves to move forward? What skills can we develop to help us manage uncertainty or cognitive dissonance, or to better read situations when we don't have all the information we would like?

Response

Think about a conflict situation in which you are currently or have recently been involved – perhaps something related to present circumstances. What questions has it given rise to, either from you or others? Use the examples from today's passage to help you examine these. Does this help you to see the questions or responses in a different light? Is there anything from this exercise which can help you move forward in this situation, or be better prepared to meet it should it arise again?

Prayer

Jesus –
the asker of deep questions
and the giver of sometimes
inscrutable
or uncomfortable
answers –
help us to grow in our capacity
to ask the right questions,
and our ability to live patiently
and persistently
with the difficult answers.
Amen.

Note

1 See Lent 5B for another reflection on this text (p. 153).

Wednesday of Holy Week – John 13.21–32

'Unsettling space'

Pat Bennett

Introduction

The text today is the central section of the story of the last supper cut adrift from its surroundings and presented as a 'stand alone' incident divorced from what precedes and follows it in the narrative. So, unless we already know the story, we have no idea what the 'this' which provokes Jesus' unease actually is and we are left hanging at the end: what is Judas doing? How will the disciples respond further to his exit? The effect is somewhat discombobulating – but once again this is very apposite since the passage itself contains a number of deeply unsettling moments.

Preparation

If you are able, spend some time looking at the painting *The Last Supper* by Jörg Ratgeb, a contemporary of Albrecht Dürer. The Museum Boijmans Van Beuningen in Rotterdam[1] has an image which allows you to zoom in on the details. Note down your responses to it – be those physical, emotional or intellectual.

Comment

The third of our readings for Holy Week brings us into a somewhat disturbed and disturbing space. The setting is a communal meal – something which Jesus and his disciples must have done on many occasions – and hence a commonplace occurrence which should have felt like a comfortable and familiar space for them. Instead, we encounter disturbing undercurrents which bring to the surface a strange mix of tension, under-standing, incomprehension, action and passivity. In fact, the whole story constitutes a deeply unsettling space.

First, there is the agitation of Jesus himself: *tarassō* conveys a strong sense of being shaken. This is not the first time we have seen Jesus in its grip – the word occurred in yesterday's passage (John 12.27) – and once again this seems to have been inaugurated by something that Jesus himself has just said. In this instance the precipitating thing (missing from today's text) is Jesus' acute awareness that a close and loved companion is about to commit a destructive act.

Whether Jesus is shaken by fear, anger or even perhaps with sorrow on behalf of, or compassion for, Judas – we simply don't know. What we can say, though, is that John is not showing us a calm and collected Jesus, protected from life by his divinity, but rather a deeply incarnated person in the grip of strong, complex and very human emotions.

Then there is the uncertainty of the disciples who manifestly have no idea what Jesus is talking about. Peter, the master fisherman, engineers the casting of line but they are then totally unable to get to grips with the fish they land! And so finally to perhaps the most unsettling aspect of all – the disruption and disintegration of Judas. In order to serve his various narra-tive agendas, John follows his usual course of painting Judas in a uniformly negative and hostile way as one in the grip of the devil. However, apart from one mention of the devil by Luke (22.3), the other evangelists are slightly less harsh in their treatment, with Matthew (27.3–5) even suggesting that the outcome was not what Judas had intended and that when he saw where his actions had actually led he was overcome with remorse.

Exploring the repentance and redemption of Judas is beyond our scope here. However, we can at least say that – as for many of us – the motives behind Judas' action were probably complex and may well have caused him some agonizing. It's also not too hard to imagine that this is something that Jesus would have been not just aware of, but also distressed by on Judas' behalf; perhaps this is indeed at least something behind this episode of *tarassō*, especially given that Jesus is about to precipitate the moment that decisively pushes Judas to commit to this course of action which will be so destructive for them both.

So then we have a space which is, for a number of reasons, very unsettling both for those within it and for those like ourselves viewing it from outside. But what, if anything, can we take from this to help us reflect on conflict?

One striking thing here is the contrast between the way in which Jesus and the disciples react to this disturbing space in which they find themselves. On the back of his turmoil, Jesus proactively sets in train the series of events that will bring about all that is at the root of it – betrayal, suffering, death – albeit as a necessary path. He not only recognizes and acknowledges his *dis*-ease but also examines and embraces it, and its consequences. In stark contrast, the disciples apparently do nothing with their patent unease. In fact they do worse than nothing – turning what appears to be a wilfully blind eye to both the disturbing undercurrents and their ever more overt manifestations. In the end, they opt to gloss the departure of Judas with a variety of anodyne narratives. And despite Jesus' explicit comments and actions, no one challenges Judas or follows him as he leaves the room.

This might lead us to reflect on the nature of our responses when we find ourselves in the unsettling situations that conflict often brings. Are we willing, like Jesus, to face and examine that inner turmoil, in order to learn from it and see where it leads; or are we more likely to follow the disciples and try to muffle it or turn a blind eye to what it appears to be showing us? What are the potential dangers in each approach and what might we do to guard against these?

Response

Consider the questions raised in the paragraph above in relation to a recent situation you have been in. Do they shine a light on anything which might have happened, or offer ideas for how you might respond differently in a future scenario?

Alternatively, revisit any responses to Ratgeb's painting which were unsettling. Try to tease the roots out and follow where that takes you, noting anything that might be worth further reflection with respect to your own understandings or handling of conflict situations.

Prayer

Jesus,
you were not immune
to being disturbed or unsettled,
but you also knew
how to face those sensations
and to collect and steady yourself
so that you could press on with the journey
to which you were committed.
Help us to grow in our capacity
to meet our turmoils
and, like you,
to learn from their uncomfortable embrace
that we too
might be able to ready ourselves
to meet what lies ahead.
Amen.

Note

1 See www.boijmans.nl/en.

Maundy Thursday –
John 13.1–17, 31b–35

'Profound paradoxical space'

Pat Bennett

Introduction

The set text today gives us the familiar, rich, well-loved story of Jesus washing his disciples' feet (minus the disturbing episode we looked at yesterday) and much has been written about all the nuances and layers of meaning behind this action. There is, however, something else very striking about this story when set against the whole spread of John's passion narrative, something which gives us the opportunity to see and consider the most important inhabited space in it, and indeed in the entirety of the gospel narratives – that of Jesus in his own body.

Preparation

Those of us of a certain age and who were brought up with 'imperial' measurements will be familiar with the adage that 'you can't get a quart into a pint pot!' For those more familiar with metric measurement, a pint is 0.568 litres and a quart is 1.136 litres – hence the meaning is pretty clear. For today's preparation, find a small box (e.g. a shoe box) and a large piece of material (e.g. a sheet or a bath towel) and explore the sensation of trying to pack something into a container which is too small for it.

Alternatively, think of some Christmas carols (or hymns) which contain imagery contrasting Christ's position or experience in heaven with his experience as a baby (e.g 'Lo! within a manger lies, he who built the starry skies') and spend some time exploring those contrasts in whatever way you like.

Comment

John's passion narrative is not without physical description, but generally when he mentions action, he is talking about things done *to* Jesus (e.g. the anointings which bookend the story) or *by* others (e.g. Peter warming himself at the courtyard fire). There is none of the descriptive detail of physical suffering which we find, for example, in Luke. In John's Passion – the longest one of all the gospels – Jesus is primarily someone who *speaks* and most of the text is a reporting of these *words*.

But here, right at the central point of the passion story, John suddenly switches to giving a detailed account of Jesus' *actions*: he gets up and leaves the table; he removes a garment and ties a towel round himself; he takes a basin and pours water; he kneels down (by implication); he washes and dries feet, moving (by implication) round the table as he does so; finally, he puts on his robe again and returns to sit at the table. Until he reaches Peter there is no reported speech – only a description of the physical actions of Jesus.

This direction of our gaze towards Jesus' bodily presence presents us with an invitation to consider the Incarnation as it is experienced *by Jesus himself*. Indeed, we might understand that in this incident he is offering to the disciples and ourselves not just a theological concept to take on board or an example to follow, but a microcosmic intimation of his own experience of taking on flesh, with all its constrictions and restrictions.

In this sense I think the Incarnation represents, at one level, the most constricted space imaginable for the one experiencing it. It 'begins in a womb and ends in a tomb' – the two most confined places any of us ever inhabit. And in between these small beginning and end points, all the vigorous, expansive, uncontainable essence of God elects to be delimited by the spatial and temporal constraints of human flesh! It seems impossible to even begin to imagine what this must have felt like. But even as Jesus presents us with the ultimate example of what it is to have one's space restricted, he also shows us that this neither defines nor limits the possibilities for living, loving and acting in expansive, generous, sacrificial, joyful and creative ways. Neither does it preclude us from making space for others within our spaces, even when those spaces may seem impossibly small (something we will return to tomorrow).

Twice now in the passion readings, we have seen Jesus shaken with agitation – he knows that suffering and death probably cannot be avoided; he realizes that agency is about to be taken away from him. And yet he continues to serve and support his disciples; to give them tools for surviving and flourishing without him (albeit they don't yet recognize them); to leave them a map and compass for the onward journey; to point them towards sources of consolation and support that they can turn to in what is to follow: 'Having loved his own who were in the world, he loved them to the end' (John 13.1). Paradoxically, the space that Jesus inhabits in his earthly life is both the most restricted and the most expansive one imaginable: the quart not only fits completely into the pint pot but also cannot be contained or defined by it and so endlessly overflows it!

Often, conflict situations will, either in reality or in our perception, seem to limit the spaces – physical, emotional or intellectual – within which we can operate. The incarnate life of Jesus, constantly presented to us through the three-year lectionary cycle, shows us that there are always possibilities for creative thinking and action – even within the most seemingly restricted spaces. How then can we find ways of discovering unseen or unrecognized possibilities at those moments when we feel that the degrees of freedom within which we can operate have been curtailed? Are there questions which we can routinely ask ourselves, or techniques which we can employ, to enable us to loosen up thought or action when we feel that we have reached the limits of our understanding or capability – especially in the context of conflict scenarios?

Response

Reflect on the questions above, perhaps in connection with a conflict scenario in which you are, or have been, involved.

Alternatively, find two jugs or other containers of very different sizes and fill the larger with water. Pour it out into the smaller, observing and relishing the sensations associated with overflow – and let this simple action lead you into prayer, following wherever the Spirit takes you.

Prayer

Jesus,
our – oh so human – brother,
you above all
knew what it was
to be confined to a small space;
and you, above all,
showed how a small space,
faithfully inhabited,
is unable to limit
either love or life.
Help us to learn
how to inhabit out own smallnesses –
whatever they may look like –
in ways which are
rich, generous and expansive
as befits the life of your kingdom.
Amen.

Good Friday – John 18.1—19.42
'Relational space'

Pat Bennett

Introduction

The reading set for today, covering as it does a lengthy span of time and a multitude of different scenes, confronts us with participants in a range of emotional, mental and physical spaces. We will concentrate on one which comes near the end – a relational space holding a moment of profound presence.

Preparation

Take a large sheet of blank paper and, working through the passage, list all the different types of spaces which people occupy. You might want to also try and group them into different types, for example, physical/mental/emotional, or active/passive, or by the people involved, etc. – use whatever taxonomy makes most sense to you. If there are particular spaces which draw your attention, make a note of this for later.

Comment

This lengthy gospel reading takes us from the last supper to the tomb by way of betrayal, violence, religious trial, denial, political trial, mockery, crucifixion, callous indifference, tender concern, death, bravery and reverence. In the course of this journey we pass through or by many different spaces inhabited by the characters we encounter. There are spaces marked or dominated by violence (e.g. Gethsemane, Pilate's courtyard, Golgotha); spaces in which people are trapped – either by their own intentions/actions or by those of others (e.g. Judas, Annas,

Caiaphas, Peter, Pilate); spaces dominated by competing narratives (the courtyard of Pilate's headquarters – on several different occasions); spaces shaped by religious or political fear (the trial scenes); spaces revealing ordinary human needs and fears (Peter in the garden and the courtyard); places of callous indifference – or maybe simply self-protection (the soldiers at various points); places revealing profound relational generosity (as Jesus is dying); places full of grief and endurance (the three Marys and John); places requiring courage (Jesus throughout, and Nicodemus and Joseph – whom we will consider in tomorrow's reflection).

Any of these might furnish us with useful tools for reflecting on the different dynamics and effects of conflict. However, the one I want to give attention to today is the one that happens in verses 26 and 27: 'When Jesus saw his mother and the disciple whom he loved standing beside her, he said to his mother, "Woman, here is your son." Then he said to the disciple, "Here is your mother." And from that hour the disciple took her into his own home.'

In a profound and deeply moving way, this moment is perhaps the ultimate paradigmatic example of what we were considering yesterday: Jesus, in the most agonizing way possible, is experiencing the confines imposed by temporality and mortality; his divinity is no protection against the physical, mental, emotional and spiritual noise to which he is being subjected in these last moments of his earthly life. Yet despite this ultimate experience of restriction, this maximum compression of his own space, Jesus reaches out to open up a beautiful, tender space of compassion and connection through which to provide immediate (and ongoing) shelter for the person within whom he himself had his first – and most life-giving – experience of confinement.

Jesus is, in this instant, fully present with his mother – just as he will also be fully present when he speaks with the dying thief in Luke's account of the scene (Luke 23.42–43). He not only recognizes and responds to her immediate relational needs, he also takes steps to affirm the importance of these and to make future provision for them to be met when he can no longer do so himself. Thus, right to the end, Jesus remains faithfully available to those around him. In this ultimate instance, it requires that he somehow muffle and restrain the clamour of his own *extremis* in order to preserve a space in which the Other can be held, connected with and sheltered. It is almost inconceivable to us that this is possible and yet Jesus does it not once, but twice – not because his divinity gives him superhuman power, but because his whole life has been lived out of this narrative centre of hospitality towards, and care for, the other – the ultimate example of the *disponibilité*[1] and creative fidelity of which the philosopher Gabriel Marcel writes so powerfully.

It is difficult to say anything in the face of this most profound moment, other than to reiterate that attention to the life of Jesus will show us how to occupy the spaces of our own lives – even in the midst of conflict – in ways which reflect the love, generosity and compassionate care which are the hallmarks of kingdom life.

Response

Simply sit with this moment and let it lead you into prayer.

Later in the day, if time permits, you might want to visit some of the spaces or groups of spaces which you identified in the preparation or which are indicated in the reflection and use these as lenses through which to reflect on your own experiences and understandings of conflict.

Prayer

Jesus,
sometimes
there
simply
are
no
words

Note

1 The word is usually translated as 'availability', but this fails to do justice to the richly textured nature of Marcel's concept. For further reading, see Gabriel Marcel, *Creative Fidelity* (New York: Fordham University Press, 2002).

Holy Saturday – John 19.38–42
'Courageous space'

Pat Bennett

Introduction

Today's reading brings us into contact with two men – one who only appears in the passion narratives and one whom we know has previously had a significant encounter with Jesus. It seems that they were both on a similar journey, though possibly at different stages. Whatever the precise truth of that, we know enough from what John says here to understand that the actions they undertake in this vignette are not without risk to their social and religious reputations and positions.

Preparation

We often use the words courage and bravery interchangeably. How would you define each word and is there a difference between them? If there is, does it matter, and if so, then why? Explore these questions in any way you find helpful.

Comment

There are a various legends attached to Joseph of Arimathea, including ones that have him bringing Christianity, vials of blood and sweat from Jesus, or even an adolescent Christ himself, to the shores of Great Britain. In contrast, the gospel accounts are somewhat sparer in their details – we know from Matthew that he was wealthy (Matt. 27.57), from Luke that he was a righteous man who was a member of the Sanhedrin (Luke 23.51) and from Mark that he was respected member of that Council (Mark 15.43). Mark and Luke also note that he was someone who 'was waiting expectantly for the kingdom of God' – so perhaps his interest in Jesus is not totally surprising.

What is less clear is the extent to which this was something about which he kept largely silent. Thus, whereas Matthew labels him 'a disciple of Jesus' (though with no comment on how open this was), John states unambiguously that his discipleship was secret 'because of his fear of the Jews'. Whatever the extent to which he was or was not a public follower of Jesus, it is clear from Luke 23.51 that he had neither agreed with, nor consented to, the actions that the Sanhedrin had taken against Jesus.

Nicodemus is a wealthy Pharisee whom John initially introduces to us at an early stage in Jesus' ministry (John 3.1–21). At that point, though clearly interested in Jesus, he is also extremely cautious about approaching him openly, coming instead under cover of darkness. Moreover, though a knowledgeable and learned man, he seems completely unable or unwilling at that point to take on board what Jesus is saying. As far as we know from the text, he slips away back into the darkness and that's the end of it. However, when we next encounter him, he is speaking up for Jesus – albeit in a somewhat oblique way – and in so doing draws a slightly sharp sarcastic response from some of his fellow Pharisees (John 7.51–52). And finally, in this passage, he comes openly to attend to the burial of Jesus, bringing costly spices.

It seems then that both of these men are on a journey towards allowing themselves to be more openly linked to Jesus. And while their wealth was unlikely to be threatened by such an association, it is clear that they both had something substantial to lose when it came to their status and reputation within the religious communities of which they were prominent members. That risk would have been even more heightened following the events of the preceding 12 hours and the persisting anxieties around the body of Jesus for those who had engineered his death (Matt. 27.62–66). Nevertheless, both men publicly associate themselves with this despised and disputed body – Joseph not only openly asking for it but also placing it in his own tomb and Nicodemus bringing expensive spices in a quantity which was anything but discrete. Neither of these are gestures that can be read as neutral or cautious!

Although we tend to view courage and bravery as synonymous, they have different etymological roots and thus each has in fact a somewhat different feel. Whereas 'brave' has its roots in Middle French and Italian words meaning bold (originally 'wild/savage'), 'courage' is, via Middle English, rooted in the French and Latin words for heart. We might perhaps think of bravery as something instinctive – running towards danger to try and save people – and courage as involving a more conscious element of choice – electing to enter the high-risk occupations such as firefighting or the Lifeboat service. In this story, Joseph and Nicodemus are aware of the risks and, while in the past they might have turned away from these and elected to stay hidden and safe, here they choose to act in defiance of them in order to honour and care for the body of Jesus.

While situations of conflict may sometimes require bravery, they almost invariably require courage of some kind. This may be the courage to risk doing something differently, or to reach out across a divide; it may be the courage to say things or take actions which might make us look foolish, or expose us to potential reputational damage; or we may need to find the courage to step outside of the narratives and understandings which give us our sense of identity and security; or to examine our own choices and actions to see if these need to be changed. Such courage might not necessarily involve us making big or dramatic gestures, or stepping out over the abyss (though it sometimes may) – but what it does require is a willingness to try and live out of the heart, just as Jesus invariably did, and just as Joseph and Nicodemus do in today's gospel passage.

Response

Think of a situation in which you have been involved that required courage in some way – either from you or from someone else. What did that look like? Are there ways in which we can encourage one another to live more courageously? Is that something which you could do more of, or would like someone to do for you? How might you personally go about this?

Prayer

The prayer for courage from the Corrymeela Community seems very apt for this story:

Courage comes from the heart
and we are always welcomed by God,
the *Croí*[1] of all being.
We bear witness to our faith,
knowing that we are called
to live lives of courage, love and reconciliation
in the ordinary and extraordinary moments
of each day.
We bear witness, too, to our failures
and our complicity in the fractures of our world.
May we be courageous today.
May we learn today.
May we love today.
Amen.

Note

1 *Croí* – pronounced 'kree' – is the Irish word for 'heart'. Prayer used with permission.

Resurrection of the Lord Year A – Matthew 28.1–10

'Disrupted space'

Pat Bennett

Introduction

Mary Magdalene and Mary, those faithful women who had stayed with Jesus as he died and then been sidelined as he was buried, take the first opportunity they can after the suspended space of the sabbath to come to the tomb and tend his body. They expect to find a sealed space – indeed their major concern in Mark's parallel account is how they will gain access to the body, since they themselves are physically incapable of removing the stone which seals the tomb (Mark 16.3). And in this version of the story, that is indeed what they find – even though, it seems, Jesus is already gone from within its confines.

Comment

In the parallel accounts of Mark, Luke and John, the stone has already been removed and Jesus has gone from the tomb before the women arrive. However, Matthew gives a slightly different version – and in so doing he alerts us to an important fact about the disruption of the space which has held the body of Jesus and with it a paradox which provides a helpful lens for thinking about conflict.

When the women arrive in this version, the stone is still firmly in place and hence we might think that Jesus is, as yet, un-risen. However, what happens on their arrival decisively gives the lie to this. There is an earthquake as an angel rolls back the stone before their eyes, an event which causes the guards to faint with terror. We might expect that this dramatic moment of opening would be followed in swift order by the emergence of Jesus himself – but no! As the angel's words make clear, Jesus was already gone from behind the sealing stone: 'He is not here; for he has been raised, as he said.'

The tomb with its rolled-away stone is one of the most vivid images in the Easter story and the centrepiece of any Easter garden. Our reflex assumption is that the stone is removed in order for Jesus to come out – after all that would make sense in human terms – and that the confining space of the tomb is shattered and disrupted by the moment of resurrection itself. However, Matthew's account suggests that we need to think about this the other way round: the disruption does not come from the inside, but from the outside. The stone is not rolled away to let Jesus out, but to let the witnesses in! The women, and later the disciples, see the empty tomb and begin, even if only slowly, to understand. Apparently, they need to see the empty tomb before they can encounter the risen Jesus. The pattern is repeated in different ways in the other gospel accounts – and in the shorter ending of Mark, the women never actually see the risen Christ, only the empty tomb. It seems that there was something particularly potent about being able to go into the space and find it different to how they had imagined.

In conflict situations too, the disruption of closed spaces may also sometimes be necessary before progress in understanding can be made. The temptation here, of course, is to reflexly assign this necessity in directions other than towards ourselves: we immediately think of all the things we perceive as 'closed spaces' belonging to other people or groups which annoy or thwart us and rush to set about them with the mental equivalent of a lump hammer! However, we ought perhaps to think first about the nature of some of our own narratives or practices, and of whether it might in fact be *they* which are hindering progress towards resolution in particular situations. If that is so, then how can we go about opening up, or more vigorously disrupting these closed spaces in ways which enable progress in understanding and ultimately changes in thinking and action? What might be the dangers of this and how could we guard against them? If necessary, how can we encourage others to open up their closed spaces? What might be some of the dangers here and how might we guard against them?

Response

Take some time to recall and revisit an occasion in your own experience (it need not necessarily be one involving conflict) where progress in resolving an issue was either impeded by a closed space, which prevented proper or deeper understandings and connections; or facilitated when somebody was able to allow a closer look into their own understandings or practices. Is there anything you can learn from this which might help you develop your own understandings of, or skills in dealing with, this type of thing in the context of a conflict situation? How might you become more aware of spaces in your own life which would benefit from a little disruption?

Prayer

Jesus
you knew when and how
to disturb and disrupt –
not in pursuit of destruction
but in the service of building
    better understanding
    deeper faith
    stronger connections.
Gift us a like wisdom
to recognize those places in our lives
which need to be broken open
in order for new life to take hold.
Amen.

The Resurrection of the Lord

John's account of the resurrection is a set text in all three years, with those of Matthew, Mark and Luke offered as alternatives in years A, B and C respectively. This section contains one reflection on each of the Johannine, Marcan and Lucan narratives; the reflection on Matthew can be found as part of the themed Holy Week set in the preceding section.

The set reading for Easter Evening is the same across all three years. Two reflections are offered here with an additional two on the gospel reading set for Easter 2 (John 20.19–31), which is also often used on Easter Evening.

Resurrection of the Lord Years A, B, C – John 20.1–18

Sarah Hills

Introduction

We have journeyed through Holy Week, from the false triumph of Palm Sunday through a garden of violence to a hill of death. We now find ourselves in a garden at Jesus' tomb. On Good Friday we journeyed with relationships of confusion, disappointment and misunderstanding which became full of fear, hate and murderous intent. Now we meet grief, astonishment, belief and ultimately understanding.

Comment

I would like to start with a story of a peace walk, which takes us from Good Friday through to Easter Day. We cannot have one without the other.

The walk took place in northern Iraq a few years ago. About 20 of us from Europe walked with local Iraqi Christians, Muslims and Yazidis, many of them internally displaced refugees. We walked for peace, to proclaim the possibility of peace in that fought-over space. On Good Friday we visited a village about 30km from Mosul – a village that had been destroyed by ISIS, the villagers having all fled or worse. It was a place of destruction, completely devoid of life. Houses were rubble, shops damaged and the church, though still standing, had been desecrated, the altar broken and lying in rubble (Photo 1, p. 260). We could hear Mosul being shelled.

We held a Good Friday service in that desecrated church. We laid candles that we had brought with us in the shape of a cross in front of the destroyed altar and prayed the prayers of

Good Friday, prayers for healing, for the end to that conflict, for peace (Photo 2).

On Easter Day, we returned to that deserted village and desecrated church. But this time, the bleakness in the church was transformed. The same rubble was there, the same bullet holes in the walls, the same broken crosses and hacked memorials. But there were people from the surrounding villages, flowers on the altar, children dressed in white and a packed church, there to proclaim the hope of the resurrection, the hope of peace and the possibility of rebuilding. The local Peshmerga, the soldiers, came to receive their Easter communion (Photo 3). There were even painted eggs and chocolate after the service. The foundation of a rebuilt community was born that day.

It was, in many ways, an extraordinary walk. Risky, at times truly dangerous. As we left that church in the destroyed village, we had to walk carefully for fear of unexploded ordinances just off the path. But in that unexpected and risky journey, we met the face of Christ in the other.

Mary Magdalene at the tomb in the garden saw the face of Christ. She believed that he was there with her. 'I have seen the Lord,' she told the others. Isn't that what the resurrection is? The acknowledgement that grief and astonishment can be transformed into belief and the ultimate understanding that love overcomes everything. 'I have seen the Lord' – Alleluia, amen!

Response

Can we believe that we too have seen the Lord? What difference will it make to how we live in difficult times?

Prayer

As we reflect on the photos of the desecrated church in Iraq, the journey from Good Friday to Easter Day – the rubble altar, the prayers for Good Friday and the bread of Christ on

the altar on Easter Day – so we pray for reconciliation and
love for all God's people.
Christ is risen. He is risen indeed!
Alleluia, Amen.

Resurrection of the Lord Year B – Mark 16.1–8

Fiona Bullock

Introduction

From the darkness of Holy Saturday, we enter the first light of Easter morning with Mary Magdalene, Mary and Salome. However, in the short ending to Mark's Gospel, this is not a scene of unbridled joy and wonder but one of utter fear. They arrive at the tomb talking together about the practicalities of the task ahead of them but they leave in silence. They come prepared with spices to anoint the dead body of Jesus but they leave unprepared for what will come next. The sun may have begun to rise in the sky but they were still to be found in the darkness of grief and from there were flung into the confusion of fear. This is a story of reality which conflicts with expectation.

In the midst of this, these women are true to their emotions and their experience is authentic. As you read the passage, become aware of the emotions you sense in them and in yourself.

Comment

According to the shorter end of Mark, the women went to the tomb so that they could do what women were expected to do. They got scared and they ran away, never to tell the story – and we have to wait for the men to arrive in another gospel before the good news of the resurrection of Jesus could be shared with many – or at least that's what it can look like!

I lived with this text for ages before I realized that this rather prejudiced view of Mark's account of Easter morning was one

I had actually adopted. It makes me ashamed to admit this as a woman. Acknowledging and naming this has allowed me to read this passage from a fresh point of view. These women were not weak and pathetic, as this account might suggest: they were willing to do their duty, to ask for help and to experience the authenticity of their feelings.

While it may have been the common practice of the time for the women to prepare the body after death, let's not shy away from the horror of what they had to face: Jesus had been beaten, whipped and had a crown of thorns forced down on his head; he had hung on the cross for hours, bleeding and in agony. There was no time to prepare his body before the sabbath and so, days after he had died, the women went to the tomb to anoint a body that was already in the first stages of decay – a brave act showing their sheer strength of character and the love they had for Jesus.

As they arrived at the tomb, they were talking and discussing who would move away the stone for them. We might assume that they were seeking a man to do the heavy lifting for them. Perhaps this was the case. Then again, there might have been an especially strong woman in the village. Regardless of who they may have had in mind, it seems that they were willing to ask for help. It takes a strong person to acknowledge that they can't do everything alone and to lean on others.

However, for me, the greatest show of strength in this passage is the women's refusal to allow someone else to tell them how to feel. The young man said to them, 'Do not be alarmed' – just as angels throughout our Scriptures have told many, 'Do not be afraid.' The women weren't alarmed, they were terrified. What on earth was going on? In my eagerness to hear the words of the young man proclaiming that Jesus had risen, I had always completely ignored Mary Magdalene, Mary and Salome. They had built themselves up to do a horrible job and they went together to support one another. When they got there, they realized that they were not fully prepared, and after all that, a stranger was sitting in the tomb telling them not to be frightened. Are you kidding me? Of course they were scared out of their wits!

Did that young man honestly think that his words would have the desired effect? Have you ever received a phone call that began with the words, 'Don't worry but …'? What was your immediate response? I think it's likely that that was the moment you began to worry.

In the pit of grief and despair, these three brave women went to the tomb and what they found there scared them. Despite the young man's instruction, they owned their feelings in that moment and beyond and I've got to say – I love them for it. They show us that our emotions cannot simply be switched off. We cannot easily detach ourselves from them. They allowed themselves to experience fear and to act upon it, choosing to keep the young man's words to themselves.

Through mental health issues, toxic relationships and spiritual turmoil, no one has the right to dictate how we feel. If we acknowledge our emotions, like our prejudices, we can explore where they have come from and how we choose to respond to them. They are part of our authentic experience and we should not dismiss them. It is important to recognize when we need to speak about our feelings with others to help us process them. Mary Magdalene, Mary and Salome were sad, grieving, hurt, disappointed and then very fearful. They didn't pretend, they didn't cover it up and it did not make them weak. They lived out a real experience, like the strong, courageous females they were and, in so doing, they encourage us to reconnect with our true emotions.

Response

Take some time to explore how you are feeling today using one of these suggestions:

- Look at the range of emojis available on your mobile phone or tablet. Can you pick out one that shows how you are feeling today? If one does not describe it fully, how many would you choose?

- Read Psalm 22. In response, compose your own psalm to express the emotions you are experiencing.
- Paint the way you feel, using oils, pastels, watercolours, poster paint or even water. Let the brush strokes become a way of articulating anything you cannot express in words.

Have your emotional responses ever been dismissed? How did you feel? Is this something you have ever done to someone else? How can we be more careful about not dismissing the emotions of others?

Prayer

We give thanks, Lord, for Mary Magdalene, Mary and Salome and for their ministry to us, showing us the importance of acknowledging how we feel, even when others try to dictate our emotions to us.
Help us to own our authentic experiences and responses as wonderful individuals created by you. Grant us the sensitivity and patience to listen to the feelings of others, especially when they differ from our own.
Amen.

Resurrection of the Lord Year C – Luke 24.1–12

Pádraig Ó Tuama

Introduction

Conflict is often itself riven with conflict. It seems obvious to say but it's worthwhile reflecting on. Conflict opens up conflicted stories about the truth. Something happens that has caused a rift and then the question is, 'What happened?'

People are believed and not believed. Some people are not believed because of facts. Some people are not believed because of the kind of people others think they are. Sometimes the truth comes in a way that disrupts the power of those who wish the truth to be a certain way.

In all of these experiences, the resurrection comes as an invitation to surprise. And as scandal.

As we mark Easter Sunday, our prayer is that we can move into truth – with all its reforming power.

Comment

What is it like to not be believed? I imagine that most people have had some experience of this; and others have had lifetimes of it.

At school, people know the experience of not being believed. Someone does something, and someone needs to account for it, and someone is not believed.

Small injustices can simply be a mirror for the larger injustices of a world: in a family, a society, a power system where the insights of some are blatantly rejected because of pre-determined prejudices. There are all kinds of reasons why a person is not believed: you're too young; you're too female; you're too gay; you're the wrong colour; you're the wrong age; you're the wrong social status; you're the wrong educational status; you're the wrong.

In the economy of Easter Sunday, it is both the form and the content of resurrection that is shocking:

The content: that love might be as big as this.
The form: that love might be as challenging as this.

In the resurrection story, the male disciples were invited into an eternal truth that required them to fundamentally change the way they saw temporal power: women's testimony was considered an idle tale. And they were products of their time and place, so they operated within the imaginative strictures of this era. In order to pay attention to the invitation of the gospel, they must amend their associations of power and their practices of disempowering in the here-and-now.

We see the same revolution happening in the fifth-century text named 'The Gospel of Mary Magdalene'. In the ninth chapter, read how the notion of holy testimony from a woman is being discussed:

When Mary had said this, she fell silent, since it was to this point that the Saviour had spoken with her. But Andrew answered and said to the brethren, 'Say what you wish to say about what she has said. I at least do not believe that the Saviour said this. For certainly these teachings are strange ideas.' Peter answered and spoke concerning these same things. He questioned them about the Saviour: Did He really speak privately with a woman and not openly to us? Are we to turn about and all listen to her? Did He prefer her to us? Then Mary wept and said to Peter, 'My brother Peter, what do you think? Do you think that I have thought this up myself in my heart, or that I am lying about the Saviour?' Levi answered and said to Peter, 'Peter you have always been hot tempered. Now I see you contending against the woman like the adversaries. But if the Saviour made her worthy, who are you indeed to reject her? Surely the Saviour knows her very well. That is why He loved her more than us. Rather let us be ashamed and put on the perfect Man, and separate as He commanded us and preach the gospel, not laying down any other rule or other law beyond what the Saviour said.' And when they heard this they began to go forth to proclaim and to preach.

Today's gospel invites all of us to consider our relationship to change, truth and personhood. Are we opposed to hearing things from certain groups of people? Wherever those corners are, it is likely we will find God there, resurrecting today, with an invitation towards a new form of power and love.

Friends, a happy and a holy Easter to you; may we all be brought more and more into the beloved community.

Response

Lent is so often a time for giving up things and also for taking up things. As we are finishing Lent, consider what Easter practices might be of benefit:

- Taking up a practice of self-reflection when you find yourself disbelieving someone; or taking up the practice of resurrection when you find yourself being disbelieved.
- Telling people you believe them might open up stories of hope and survival that have been long hidden, waiting for the trusting light of kindness.

Let us let an Easter light shine into the way we respond to people.

Prayer

Surprising Son of God
you revealed the truth to women
who were not believed by men.

You are in the voices of the unbelieved
and the ignored.
So bring us towards each other.
Bring us towards
the truest truth.
Because here, if anywhere,
will we find you.
Amen.

Easter Evening – Luke 24.13–49

Fiona Bullock

Introduction

As one of the first encounters with Jesus following his resurrection, this is a story of wonder and joy. Cleopas and his friend don't immediately recognize Jesus and it is only later, once he has accepted the hospitality they offer and has broken bread with them, that they come to know him. On the way to that moment of recognition, Jesus also gives them, and us, a masterclass in how to walk alongside others.

Preparation

As you read the passage, consider how it might guide us to have more healthy interactions and dialogue with one another. What does this encounter have to teach us about sharing our stories and listening to the stories of others?

Comment

In the midst of conflict, engaging in dialogue enables participants to tell their story and to listen to the stories of others. People can experience the empowering effect of having their voice heard and in turn have the opportunity to show respect and compassion by listening thoughtfully to others. The story of the Emmaus encounter gives us some pointers towards creating a safe space for dialogue which may prove to be helpful for our everyday conversations as well as for use in situations of conflict.

1 *Jesus walked alongside Cleopas and his companion*

Jesus showed his willingness to walk with them for a while. While we need to think about how to do this safely and sensitively in a conflict situation, it is productive to be willing to step into someone else's shoes and consider what their perspective might be. Engaging in dialogue shows a desire to journey with others to a new point of respect and understanding. It is therefore important to be fully present and to expect dialogue to continue beyond one encounter.

2 *Jesus used an open question: 'What are you discussing?'*

Rather than indicating that he'd probably heard much of their conversation, he invited them to share with him what they wished. He didn't lead their answer in a particular direction and they certainly could not answer with just 'yes' or 'no'. The types of questions we ask one another can directly affect the tone and course of a discussion. If they are open and measured, without prejudice or antagonism, it facilitates a conversation between equals who want to learn about similarities, differences and ways of moving forward.

3 *When they gave a sharp retort, Jesus did not rise to it*

'Are you the only stranger in Jerusalem who does not know the things that have taken place there in these days?' – reads as an accusation, whether of ignorance or stupidity is not clear. However, Jesus does not retaliate or react in kind. Instead, he asks his question again. He does not get side-tracked or drawn into a petty squabble but retains a neutral stance by sticking to his open question. Sometimes in life, when it comes to inconsequential little things, we have to be prepared to just 'let it go'.

4 *Jesus listened without judgement*

He allowed them the space and the opportunity to share their story without judgement or criticism. He honoured their story by not interrupting them or correcting their information. We do not often have the opportunity to tell our story from beginning to end. This experience is empowering and allows us to hear the content of what we are saying and the manner in which we are expressing ourselves. On occasion, saying aloud how we feel can cause us to reflect on our words or behaviours and consider modifying them.

5 Only when they had finished telling their story did Jesus respond by telling his

Cleopas and his companion were given the space to tell their story their way. When they had finished, Jesus took this as his cue to speak. Although his first words in response may seem rude – 'How foolish you are' – an analysis of the Greek can help us reach a different conclusion. The Greek word *anoetoi* is used here, the nuance of which suggests that Jesus was commenting that they had come to their conclusion without applying reason. They had been thoughtless in their application of the scriptures and had demonstrated a lack of faith in the prophecies written there. From this point, they walked alongside him as he patiently taught them his version of events and they listened. Each party had an opportunity to speak and to be heard, which showed that all were valued. In dialogue, as in the rest of life, we all seek reassurance that we matter.

6 They journeyed together

Not only had they travelled a fair distance on foot, they had also journeyed far in their understanding. Engaging in dialogue had helped them to set their stories within a wider context and to come to a greater understanding of themselves and others.

Dialogue begins when we are willing to step out of our comfort zones, listen compassionately, tell our stories faithfully and share respect. As we travel through life, we will encounter many people whose lived experience differs greatly from our own. We should approach one another with respect and with hope that we can learn to appreciate our differences. However, there may be times when those differences will be too great for us to find common ground, no matter how hard we try. We may find new ways to move forward, whether together or apart. We have to decide whether it is worth taking the risk of disappointment or hurt to achieve a safe place to share our stories and, potentially, a more positive journey onward.

Jesus travelled with Cleopas and his companion along the road to Emmaus and on their faith journeys. No one was left untouched by this encounter, as their lives were transformed through dialogue.

Response

Take some time to try and tune in to the soundscape where you are. Notice how difficult it can be to block out the noise of your own thoughts.

When you ask someone, 'How was your day?' be ready to follow up with a question that explores why it was a good/bad day for them. Really listen to their answer.

Be present. Put down your mobile phone when you are having a meal and talk to your companions.

Prayer

Triune God,
you call us into relationship
but you never told us how hard it could be.
Guide us to be connectors in our fractured communities.
Provide us with the words to tell our stories
and the patience to listen to the stories of others.
Prepare the way for bridges to be built, as we graft together.
Help us to let the little things go,
as we focus on loving, forgiving, inviting and accepting.
Walk with us, Lord Jesus.
Amen.

Easter Evening – Luke 24.13–35

Alex Wimberly

Introduction

In this familiar and well-loved story, the revealed and risen Jesus gets us to reconsider all we've seen and sets a fire in our hearts.

Comment

Seeing and not seeing fascinate us in this passage. The eyes of the two disciples 'were kept from recognizing' Jesus; but later, in the breaking of bread, 'their eyes were opened, and they recognized him'. Although the two consider their companion ignorant for not knowing about all the things that had recently taken place, it is Jesus who illuminates their experience in the light of his death and resurrection. As soon as they realize who is standing in front of them, Jesus vanishes 'from their sight'.

Looking back on their encounter with the risen Jesus, the disciples reassess what happened: 'Were not our hearts burning within us while he was talking?' Everything that came before is now seen in the knowledge of Jesus' resurrection – including their recent conversation with this supposed stranger.

As we continue along our current path, everything we see is being re-examined in the reality of a pandemic. What seemed normal before is being reassessed in the light of a world that has had to stop and address a global crisis. Inequalities we had ignored are now revealed as inexcusable. Healthcare and social services we took for granted are now recognized as invaluable. Workers who had never before captured our collective attention are now rightly seen as essential. And when this present crisis vanishes from our sight, we will not be able to unsee the conflicted realities that are now laid bare.

Response

As a response to this familiar but strangely urgent story, we can reconsider what the disciples meant when they said their hearts were 'burning within' them while Jesus spoke to them – and why they went back to Jerusalem with such urgency.

We can read this phrase as indicating a strange warmth, a pleasant and cosy reassurance that managed to settle the nerves of a frightened duo still trying to make sense of their trauma; as a flickering internal glow that motivated them to share heart-warming news with their friends.

But in our own context, a new burning in our hearts not only comforts us with the reassurance of Jesus' resurrection – it provides this pandemic's glaring illumination on what has been true for too long: inequality, injustice and inaction. Having our eyes opened, we see more clearly the persistence of societal and personal conflicts that cause real harm. As we re-examine everything that has come before in the light of this global crisis, we too will want to acknowledge things now evident – both the good and the bad – and hurry back to address the systemic problems we kept ourselves from seeing.

Prayer

Risen and revealing God,
you walked with us for a long time before we knew
who you truly were.
We talked about this world
as if we were the ones who saw it clearly.
Now that we more fully recognize
your continued presence with us,
give us eyes to see the beauty that surrounds us,
as well as the problems we have too long ignored.
And may our hearts then burn
with your illuminating and catalysing fire
that we might see the world that you envision.
Amen.

Easter 2 – John 20.19–31

Alex Wimberly

Introduction

In a time of fear and uncertainty, Easter surprises us with a message of peace and reconciliation.

Comment

This resurrection story contains a great deal of conflict, both implicit and explicit. Doors are locked 'for fear of the Jews', a category we might argue includes the disciples, yet is meant to distinguish them from their contemporaries. Thomas, in his doubt, sets himself apart from and against his friends and sets up a confrontation with Jesus. And then there is the peace that Jesus brings, repeatedly, because it repeatedly needs to be brought. A greeting of 'Peace be with you' implies that peace is not already present.

For those of us locked away in fear these days from one threat or another, whose blend of faith and doubt has yet to make sense of what Easter means in a post-coronavirus context, John's huddled disciples seem all the more familiar.

It is strangely easy to miss, therefore, that this is a story of reunion and resolution and of reconciliation. Fear transforms into joy in these moments. Doubt transforms into conviction through these encounters. Disagreement and confusion transform into a shared witness. This is all because a dear friend thought lost to death has returned. Whatever guilt these disciples may have felt for their abandonment of Jesus in the garden, their denying of him in the courtyard or their powerlessness in the face of death, it has all been transformed by the forgiveness found in the risen Lord's greeting: 'Peace be with you.'

Conflict and division will persist after Easter – because humanity will persist – but Easter nevertheless offers us the power to be at peace in our altered reality.

Response

Easter leads us to see our present context in a new light: one of anticipated reunion and the eventual resolution to our current crisis and with faith in the enduring power of reconciliation.

The surprise of Jesus in our midst encourages us to ask what we want a resurrected world to look like. What will transform our fears into joy? How will we change if we accept the peace that comes in knowing the power of life over death? With whom will we become reconciled once this separation is over – when we are close enough to see each other's scars and to share each other's stories?

Prayer

Risen and reconciling God,
your greeting after the grave acknowledged
the trauma and turmoil of that time and our own.
The message of peace
was what your disciples needed to hear
and what the world needs now.
When we are reunited
with those from whom we've been separated,
may our greetings, too, be of peace,
and may we see all division in the light of your reconciliation
and all crises in the context of your resurrection.
Amen.

Easter 2 – John 20.19–31

Glenn Jordan

Introduction

It's difficult to predict the impact on the body of violence experienced or witnessed. Perhaps over the centuries of interpretation, we have not given enough attention to the trauma that the disciples suffered in witnessing the final days of Jesus' life, nor to the despair at their own failures and perceived weaknesses as they deserted him. So when we find them locked into a room for fear of the outside world, we should take note of the horror of their recent experience. But nor should we miss the power, and the symbolism, of Jesus entering that locked-in state and declaring peace.

Comment

There is much to consider in just the first two verses of our reading today: 'On the evening of that first day of the week, when the disciples were together, with the doors locked for fear of the Jewish leaders ...'

First, there is the symbolism of the evening. The day has gone, the darkness is creeping in. Nature itself is in sympathy with these disciples who had seen all their plans and hopes dashed with the death of their leader. It was night, not just in the streets of Jerusalem, but in the hearts of each one in that sealed room.

And that's the second thing – they were locked in. I think there's something symbolic here too. Witnessing violence, or having violence inflicted, can have that effect. It can lock a person into their trauma. The disciples here were bolted inside that room, but locked in also to the trauma they had seen and experienced.

Tragically, many of us will have known this effect. We have witnessed violence acted out in front of us, or we have experienced violence, physically, emotionally or psychologically. Aggression and abuse can deprive us of a voice, can turn us in on ourselves and away from the rest of the world.

These days we may write about these people suffering from PTSD, the physical or psychological impact of being in a perceived life-or-death situation, or of being surrounded by violence. It can bring on anxiety or stress, fearful feelings, hallucinations, nightmares, flashbacks and panic attacks. Some experience selective mutism, where they just can't communicate. For some they avoid life, become agoraphobic or listless, or simply have an inability to communicate. Was this in the experience of the disciples just days after the crucifixion?

And third, there is the source of their fear – the Jewish leaders. This is a difficult thing to consider, yet it is a common theme within John's Gospel. Time and again he speaks about peoples' actions or words being constrained 'for fear of the Jews'. There may be some factual or historical accuracy in the account, for the people who did these things happened to be Jewish, but within days, the movement that began here in this locked-in state moved out of that room and confidently began to proclaim their message. Within 400 years it was the official religion of the empire. A thousand years later it spanned the globe.

It was, and is, no longer a minority movement in many parts of the world. In many places we are the reigning powers. How easily then, over the course of this history, did the factual statements of John's Gospel become the permissive cause for anti-Semitism. This statement here in John's Gospel, describing the actual fear experienced by those first disciples, became a generalized prejudice against a whole people group. It perhaps reached its lowest and most shameful point in the Holocaust, but it still has the power to commandeer the headlines.

How frequently do we see those who have been traumatized transfer their trauma on to another group whom they demonize and ultimately subject to the same violence and trauma that they themselves have experienced. This is an endless, violent cycle of revenge and retribution. Perpetrated from the locked room of our pain and anguish.

But the verse doesn't end there. It says, 'Jesus came and stood among them and said, "Peace be with you!"'

The risen Christ, so recently the victim of scapegoating violence, comes and stands in the midst of the locked-in room and offers a new way out of the destructive cycle of revenge and retribution. 'Peace be with you!'

That's what they needed to hear, locked in to their pain and their trauma. It is the blessing he offers in the noise and tumult of their torment. Peace!

And this was no easy peace. It was no Pollyannaish view which refuses to look at the harsh reality of a violent world. For Jesus shows them the scars on his hands and his side. This is not make-believe, this is peace in the context of real suffering and violence. Jesus still carries his scars and yet offers peace. The magnitude of this should not be underestimated.

Last Wednesday, 4 April, was the fiftieth anniversary of the assassination of Martin Luther King Jr, the great apostle of non-violence. He once said:

The ultimate weakness of violence is that it is a descending spiral, begetting the very thing it seeks to destroy. Instead of diminishing evil, it multiplies it. Through violence you may murder the liar, but you cannot murder the lie, nor establish the truth. Through violence you may murder the hater, but you do not murder hate. In fact, violence merely increases hate. So it goes. Returning violence for violence multiplies violence, adding deeper darkness to a night already devoid of stars. Darkness cannot drive out darkness: only light can do that. Hate cannot drive out hate: only love can do that.[1]

Response

Take some time to research a conflict zone in the world which you know little about. Learn something of the history of the conflict, the types of violence and the experiences of people there. What do people say about their world? What do journalists, experts and politicians say about it? What signs of trauma are present? Where are the risks of cyclical violence?

Now imagine what it would mean for Jesus to enter that scene and declare peace.

Prayer

Strong God,
who knows what it is to be a victim,
you step into the locked-in places of our world
and our lives
and declare Peace.

You do so as someone who has known trauma
and bears the scars.

Forgive us for each occasion
when we have struck out in our pain
and created new victims
alongside ourselves.

Teach us how to carry our scars
strengthen us to be receptive to your Spirit
free us from the destructive cycle of violence
for our own sake,
for our community's sake,
and for Jesus' sake,
who was an innocent victim.
Amen.

Note

1 Martin Luther King, Jr, *Where Do We Go From Here: Chaos or Community?* (Boston, MA: Beacon Press, 1967), p. 181.

Contributors

Pat Bennett

Pat is a writer and liturgist based in Glasgow. She has a dual background in science and theology and a deep interest from both perspectives in the area of interpersonal dynamics and human flourishing. She is a member of the Iona Community and previously worked for them as their Programmes Development Worker.

Fiona Bullock

Fiona is a parish minister in the Church of Scotland, having previously worked in education and health. With a background in law, peace and reconciliation, and theology, she has particular interests in peace education, reconciliation and compassionate listening.

Janet Foggie

Janet is the CEO of Community Energy Scotland, a charity that works for net zero and to end fuel poverty through community renewable energy projects. She has a background in history, theology and mediation and has worked in hospital chaplaincy, parish ministry and in community building for the Church of Scotland at the University of Stirling. She has a deep commitment to working for equality and inclusion.

Ruth Harvey

A Church of Scotland minister and a Quaker, Ruth is a trained and accredited mediator with a special interest in peace building and spiritual formation. A former director of Place for Hope, she is the current leader of the Iona Community.

Sarah Hills

Prior to ordination, Sarah practised as a psychiatrist specializing in psychotherapy. She has extensive experience in the areas of conflict and reconciliation in the national church and internationally and has been the Canon for Reconciliation at Coventry Cathedral since 2014. She is currently the vicar of Holy Island.

Glenn Jordan

Glenn was a widely respected community activist and public theologian. He was interested in the power of story to create newness and transform conflict, and brought a love of language, place, art and relationship to all his work. He was a beloved member of the Spirituality of Conflict team. He died in June 2020.

Pádraig Ó Tuama

Pádraig is a well-known poet, essayist, speaker and broadcaster with an extensive background in conflict work at local and national level. He has a passionate interest in language, poetics, conflict and storytelling, and in the application of narrative analysis to biblical texts. A former leader of the Corrymeela Community, he is currently Theologian in Residence to the On Being project, for which he also curates and presents the 'Poetry Unbound' podcast.

Brec Seaton

Brec is a trained and accredited mediator and a practitioner and trainer with Place for Hope, for whom she provides support to congregations and faith communities through times of transition and change. She also works for the British Methodist Church organizing and provisioning a wide range of learning and development opportunities for churches and church leaders, including developing training resources around conflict, scripture, bullying behaviour and domestic abuse.

Trevor Williams

Now retired, Trevor has worked in Northern Ireland for more than 30 years, as a parish priest in North Belfast, as Bishop of Limerick and Killaloe and for BBC Northern Ireland. He is also a former Chair of Christian Aid Ireland and former Leader of the Corrymeela Community. Trevor is deeply committed to, and continues to be involved in, the work of reconciliation, inter-church and inter-faith relations, community development and communications.

Alex Wimberly

Alex is the current leader of the Corrymeela Community. Originally from the USA, Alex worked as a Presbyterian minister in Belfast and as a chaplain at the Community's Ballycastle Centre prior to his appointment as Leader. He has a particular interest in how the Christian motif of reconciliation manages to be divisive, and in encouraging and supporting folk in becoming centres of peace and reconciliation wherever they live, work and worship.

Index of Biblical References

Index of Names and Subjects